THE
NAKED
CODE

THE NAKED CODE

THE SIMPLE SCIENCE BEHIND LOOKING GOOD NAKED AND WHY IT MATTERS

BRONSON TAYLOR

PUBLISHING

ADVANCED PRAISE

"The Naked Code may cause you to reevaluate everything you thought you knew about diet, exercise and weight loss. In the book, Taylor lays out a clear, actionable plan for losing weight and building muscle. It's an easy, fun read and his template is simple enough for anyone to follow."

Al Kavadlo, Author of Get Strong and Next Level Strength

"The Naked Code is the slap in the face that the fitness industry needs. It is time to stop over thinking nutrition and exercise. You don't need a fancy gym or a magical diet, this is pure common sense to the core and backed by results."

Dr. Jaime Seeman, Doctor Fit and Fabulous

"Bronson has done an excellent job at cutting through the noise to arrive at the simplest, most effective style of eating and exercising. When applied consistently, these habits will naturally result in a lean, athletic body. I can fully endorse this because my approach is very similar. If you've tried everything to get a lean, amazing body—The Naked Code will give you the answers you've been searching for."

William Shewfelt, Actor (The Red Power Ranger), Speaker, and Health Coach

"You can change your life in one afternoon. The simple approach laid out in this book is essentially the same thing I've found after 5 years of research, self-experimentation, and interviewing over 100 world-renowned leaders in the health field. It's a bit hard to believe, but being fit and healthy is as simple as The Naked Code puts forth."

Brian Sanders, Director of Food Lies

"Brilliant! Taylor wisely ignores all the health media and marketing fluff to break down achieving better health into what it should be; one simple equation. If you want to look good naked, do what he says in this book!"

Dr. Stephen Hussey, Co-owner of Resource Your Health

"The Naked Code is simple, evidence-based, effective, and could help thousands of people achieve their health and fitness goals without relying on lots of willpower, money, or time."

Scott Myslinski, Host of The Carnivore Cast

"Bronson Taylor brilliantly ties together basic carnivore nutrition and training principles with his own adventures of turning his "Dad Bod" into a "feel confident naked Bod". The Naked Code is a 'Go-To' manual for anyone looking to overhaul their health & physique. This book is a library staple for the everyday man and woman".

Dr. Nevada Gray PharmD, RN, CPT

Printed in the United States of America

First Printing, 2019

ISBN 978-0-578-57265-9

Wriote Publishing
9990 Coconut Rd.
Bonita Springs, FL 34135

bronson.taylor@gmail.com
www.bronsontaylor.com

For Megan, Mikah, Bear, and Bjørn,
who eat steak and do push-ups with me.

Visit **www.bronsontaylor.com** to join my *Really Freakin' Good* email list.

At the end of each year I send one, and only one, email. It summarizes everything I've learned, and everything I've done, in the previous 12-months. It's also the easiest way to be kept up-to-date on any new books that I write.

I promise it will be entertaining and add tremendous value to your life. Sign up now!

TABLE OF CONTENTS

INTRODUCTION
WHY I HACKED THE FITNESS INDUSTRY

I Was a Fat Founder

My career was going great as the CEO of a million-dollar tech startup, and my family was growing and thriving with three amazing sons and a loving wife, but my body had taken a back seat to all of my other responsibilities. This isn't a new story. It was a gradual decline, a few pounds a year, but it was all starting to add up in my mid-thirties. My pants were thirty-eight inches around the waist, and I was at least fifty pounds overweight. In my mind I looked like I had in high school: a thin basketball player. But the mirror didn't play along; I looked ugly naked.

Part of me wanted to start focusing on my health, but another part of me felt selfish for even thinking about my body. I had kids to feed. I had employees to support. I had a mental block. I associated health and fitness with young egocentric guys who had fewer responsibilities.

Then I had an epiphany one day after walking up a set of stairs to my office. While I was breathing unusually hard, I thought, "If I die young, who is going to take care of my wife, kids, and employees?" Cardiac disease runs in my family, and I was already overweight, so this wasn't a purely theoretical thought.

Then I had another epiphany. Looking good naked, if achieved in the right way, is an indicator of overall health. Waist size correlates with cardiac health[1], and waist size also correlates with looking good naked. Muscularity correlates with longevity[2], and muscularity also correlates with looking good naked. If I cared about those around me, I should try to look good naked. Think about it—it's not as crazy as it sounds.

---

[1] https://www.ncbi.nlm.nih.gov/pmc/articles/PMC5318865

[2] https://www.ncbi.nlm.nih.gov/pmc/articles/PMC4035379

The Failed Experiment

That's when I decided I should eat less and move more. That's the obvious thing to do, right? Eat less food and burn more calories through exercise. The experts all preach that weight loss is just that simple. They say it's all thermodynamics (calories in vs. calories out), and who am I to question a concept like *thermodynamics*? Besides, this should be easy. I'm an entrepreneur, so I know how to be ridiculously committed to something. I read *Born to Run* for proper inspiration, and I unofficially joined the cult of jogging (or as Ron Burgundy would call it, "yogging").

I tried to eat less and I ran 564.3 miles over the course of a few years. It worked incredibly well. Just kidding—I didn't lose any fat at all, and I gained no muscle. I even looked worse in the mirror. Running made me look aged and tired without improving my body composition. You read that correctly. I tracked every single mile in my Nike running app, and the whole experiment was completely pointless. I eventually found out that one of the featured runners in *Born to Run*, Micah True, died of   heart disease at age fifty-eight. He was found dead days after leaving for a twelve-mile run.[3] Want to know something even crazier? This kind of death for a runner is not uncommon. The dirty little

---

[3]https://patch.com/california/agourahills/born-to-run-ultrarunner-died-of-heart-disease-autopsy-reveals

secret of running is that there's a correlation between endurance running and heart disease.[4] In fact, the first marathoner in recorded history, Pheidippides, died in 490 BCE, directly after completing a marathon.[5] (This should have been humanity's first hint to avoid this kind of thing.) There is even a Wikipedia page[6] that tracks running deaths at marathons, and these are only the fatalities that happen at the actual marathons. Imagine all of the people who die during training and are unlisted. Runners are supposed to have an advanced, robust, and healthy cardiovascular system. That's what we all assume. Nope.

Rethinking Everything

My desire to be lean and muscular was still alive, but the *commonsense* approach to achieving this goal was completely wrong. Moving more and eating less doesn't work, and this has been shown in multiple studies.[7] That's when it occurred to me that my journey toward

---

[4] https://www.ncbi.nlm.nih.gov/pmc/articles/PMC3119133

[5] John A. Lucas. A History of the Marathon race 490 B.C. to 1975. Pennsylvania State University & Los Angeles 1984 Foundation. Retrieved 2012-04-08.

[6] https://en.wikipedia.org/wiki/List_of_marathon_fatalities

[7] https://idmprogram.com/evidence-caloric-restriction

health might be a lot like my journey in business. In the startup world there is a constant stream of terrible advice. There are so many gurus, case studies, and best practices that are filled with distortions and lies that you have to be ruthless in your search for truth.

One night, someone suggested that I drink more apple cider vinegar to improve my health, and in that moment something snapped in my brain. I started furiously searching online for peer-reviewed research papers and clinical trials involving apple cider vinegar. I was done with the witchcraft that had infiltrated the fitness industry. The voodoo wisdom that is passed from mom to mom and the bro science that is passed from dude to dude had to come to an end. No ones' life is being transformed because of apple cider vinegar. Why are we talking about apple cider vinegar?

That's when I decided to take on the fitness industry with the same set of skills that allowed me to find success in the startup world. My company had built applications that rely on artificial intelligence, machine learning, and big data, so I felt qualified to find the signal in the noise of the fitness industry. It was time to use my skills to improve my health.

I was going to crack The Naked Code.

At that time, my knowledge of health, nutrition, and exercise could have easily fit on a small napkin, so I didn't have much to start with. This was actually a huge benefit because I could go anywhere the evidence took me. There were no sacred cows in my fitness paradigm.

My goal was to discover the fitness axioms that accurately predicted body composition. I wanted to know the fundamental truths that create 90 percent of the results, not the fringe ideas that merely optimize an already working plan. I don't care about yak butter in my coffee if I'm overweight. It just doesn't move the needle. (Sorry, Bulletproof people.) I don't care about getting enough creatine, BCAA, apple cider vinegar, or whatever fad compound in my diet if I'm fat and can't do a single push-up. No amount of creatine was going to get my body back from the brink. Would creatine improve a functioning protocol? Probably. Would it be a primary reason I achieved results? Probably not.

To put it another way, I wanted to know the necessary and sufficient conditions for building muscle and losing fat. What absolutely must be present, and what is superfluous? This became the all-important question, and this mindset served as a forcing function. Whenever I considered labeling something as a non-negotiable law, I would ask the question, "Can I lose fat and gain muscle without this?" If the answer was yes, then I moved on.

After obsessive study, constant self-experimentation, large doses of ignoring the experts, and being willing to challenge the myriad of assumptions in the fitness industry, I finally found a simple code that makes humans look and feel awesome. It is deceptively short and easy to understand, but remember, truth should be simple. If E=MC² can describe the movement of galaxies, then there should be a simple equation that explains how humans can avoid getting fat while still building muscle.

Here is the code:

P>C+F 3PPKS = LEAN

The rest of this book will walk you through what this code means. It is relatively easy to follow and can be accomplished in minutes each week. Nevertheless, it will create astonishing results.

Case Studies

This code allowed me to lose fifty-eight pounds of fat and gain twenty pounds of muscle, all within a year and a half. I shared an early version of this code with my dad and within four months he reversed his type 2 diabetes, was off all of his medications (including insulin), and lost forty-two pounds. My grandmother recently went to her doctor and was also told she was a diabetic. She told her doctor that she didn't want to go on medication and that her grandson had a book she was going to follow instead. She just called to tell me that her lab results all came back normal. Her nephrologist even said her levels were the best they've been this year. My family health history is an absolute mess, and yet somehow three members of the same family are quickly turning their health around.

You may wonder how diabetes, or any disease, has anything to do with a book on looking good naked, but what I've discovered is that there is a deep connection between health and aesthetics. If we achieve our visual results the right way, we should expect our health markers to improve.

My dad, grandmother, and I are not the only ones who have found results with the information in this book. There are a few notable doctors that have radically improved the body composition and health of their patients by utilizing parts of this code. Dr. Fung[8], Dr. Naiman[9], Dr. Eades[10], and others are seeing incredible changes in their patients, but they aren't prescribing the typical advice of other doctors. Their medical advice is based on contemporary science, and this has profoundly influenced my thinking.

Dr. Ted Naiman, a family physician in Seattle for over twenty years, said, "It has been phenomenally

---

[8] https://idmprogram.com

[9] https://www.virginiamason.org/ted-naiman-md

[10] https://proteinpower.com/drmike

rewarding. I have a huge number of patients, hundreds, who have lost 50, 100, or 150 pounds (23-68 kg). I have countless people who have completely reversed their diabetes.

I have seen migraines, anorexia, infertility, fibromyalgia, rheumatoid arthritis, psoriasis, asthma, acne—even more diseases—all greatly improve, even cured, on this diet. Mental health issues like bipolar, depression, anxiety, OCD, all get much better, too."

This patient data is important because it validates the scientific studies referenced throughout this book. Anyone can read a study, misinterpret the causal agent, and think they are justified in some strange belief. However, if that belief enters the real world and fails, it's a signal that something is missing in our understanding. When peer-reviewed research aligns with observation and experience, then we are getting close to the truth.

Dr. Naiman's practice shows that the conclusions reached in this book are grounded in reality and will produce results for the everyday person. It's worth noting that much of the dietary advice in this book is based off the work of Dr. Ted Naiman, and I want him to get full credit for these ideas. The protein/energy ratio concept comes directly from Dr. Naiman.

This is not a book of theory. This is a book that can completely change the trajectory of your health, and how you look. There are four main reasons why The Naked Code works so well:

1. **Data**: The Naked Code is based on decades of patient encounters and hundreds of transformed lives.

2. **Logic**: The Naked Code exposes the errors in the most widely believed concepts concerning weight loss and muscle gain.

3. **Science**: The Naked Code is based on over twenty peer-reviewed studies, which are cited throughout this book.

4. **Math**: The Naked Code reduces everything down to a simple equation that is easy to understand, remember, and follow.

Who Is The Naked Code For?

Will this code work for most people? Yes. Will it work for everyone? Probably not. However, this isn't because of some fundamental flaw in its design, but because there are always outliers on any standard bell curve.[11] It's been documented that some people get drowsy by ingesting

---

[11] http://www.allanbesselink.com/blog/smart/528-the-bell-curve-outliers-and-training-myths

caffeine.[12] Does this mean that it's a lie to say that caffeine gives you energy? I don't think we need to qualify our language for the sake of a few edge cases. I'm not going to hedge my statements throughout this book because there is someone who gets tired when drinking coffee, or someone who doesn't respond positively to The Naked Code. In most situations most of the time with most people, what I am recommending will work better than any alternative.

On a similar note, is The Naked Code the only way to get results? Of course not. Some people are on the opposite end of the bell curve I mentioned above, and their superior genetics will allow them to find positive results with almost any method they follow. If you have won the genetic lottery, feel free to put this book down. You'll find results doing anything or nothing, or even in spite of what you are doing. However, if you are just a regular person, like me, then keep reading.

With those caveats out of the way, I think The Naked Code will work for more people than any other exercise or diet routine. It is simpler to understand than the alternatives, it requires far less time and money than expected, and it will make you very happy with how you look and feel.

The Naked Code also works because it doesn't just show you how to lose weight, or just show you how to

---

[12] https://www.healthline.com/health/food-nutrition/coffee-makes-me-tired

build muscle. It does both. This is important because looking good naked requires having a low body fat percentage while also building muscle (this is true for men and women).

Some women are afraid of building muscle because they don't want to look bulky. The reality is that building muscle is difficult for men and extremely difficult for women. If you are a woman, and you are not taking steroids, your training will simply make you look healthy and fit, nothing more.

So, are you ready to unlock The Naked Code? Are you ready to look good with your clothes off?

The photo on the left was taken in June of 2017 (age thirty-four) when I got my passport renewed before my trip to Vancouver.

The photo on the right was taken in June of 2019 (age thirty-six) when I got my Costa Rican driver's license before my trip to Costa Rica.

These photos were taken exactly two years apart. I wanted to use these photos as my before and after face photos because then it isn't about me finding the worst photo from before and the best photo after and comparing them. This is how I actually looked on a random day with only one photo taken.

The photo on the left was taken in the summer of 2016 (age thirty-three) when I lived in Chicago for the summer (I was playing in the pool with my kids). I was fat with almost no muscle (I couldn't do a single push-up).

The photo on the right was taken in the summer of 2019 (age thirty-six) when I lived in Costa Rica. I have completely overhauled my body during my mid-thirties.

CHAPTER 1

THE GOLDEN RATIO FOR FAT LOSS

The Truth About Fat

Repeat after me: Food dictates fat loss. Exercise dictates muscle gain. Food dictates fat loss. Exercise dictates muscle gain. Food dictates fat loss. Exercise dictates muscle gain.

This means that exercising to lose fat will not work. Likewise, eating to build muscle will not work. Muscle and fat represent different biological systems. It is ideal to do both, but there are plenty of muscular people who are fat (just watch a strongman competition on TV when you are bored one night). Likewise, there are plenty of skinny people who are not muscular (just watch *America's Next Top Model* on TV one night when you are really, really, super bored). If weight loss and muscle gain were the same system, based on the same inputs and outputs, then muscle gain and fat loss would correlate in humans, but they don't.

You're probably wondering how food dictates fat loss (we'll get to muscle gain in the second part of this book), but first, I need to debunk the most pervasive and terrible advice that the fitness industry has hoisted upon us, the theory that almost everyone believes will lead to fat loss. I'm talking, of course, about "moving more and eating less." This theory also goes by the following names and phrases: calories in, calories out (CICO), the energy expenditure equation, the calorie theory of obesity, and thermodynamics. Ask any random person how to lose weight and they'll say, "You just need to eat less food and exercise more. Duh!" Michelle Obama's health initiative was even called "Let's Move!"

This theory basically suggests that if someone's daily caloric need is 2,000 calories, and a pound of fat is equal to 3,500 calories, then the math looks something like this:

Day	Calories In	Calories Out	Change
Monday	2,000	2,000	0 pounds
Tuesday	2,500	2,000	+1/7 pounds
Wednesday	1,000	2,500	-3/7 pounds
Total	**5,500**	**6,500**	**-2/7 pounds**

There are two reasons why this is wrong. The first reason is that you cannot realistically change the "calories out" part of this equation, and the second reason is that you cannot realistically change the "calories in" part of this equation either. If these variables were malleable, we could effectively change our weight by manipulating our caloric intake and output, but unfortunately it's not that straightforward. We'll start by looking at the difficulties of changing our "calories out."

If a pound of fat is equal to approximately 3,500 calories[13], then you must burn an extra 3,500 calories during an activity to lose one pound. A 200-pound person burns about 150 calories by running a mile.[14] It's just math at this point. You would need to run twenty-three miles to lose one pound. Oh, and don't forget to avoid *working up an appetite* while you run this incredible distance. You don't want to throw away all of your progress with one indulgent meal.

I assure you that whatever you are currently doing for exercise is an absolute joke (in terms of calories burned) compared to running twenty-three miles. Your treadmill, Pilates, yoga, jazzercise, power walking, Tae Bo, or whateverridiculousthingtheydreamupnext™ will

---

[13] https://academic.oup.com/ajcn/article-abstract/6/5/542/4729975

[14] https://caloriesburnedhq.com/calories-burned-running

not help you get rid of the fat on your body. Sweating and breathing hard does not equal fat loss.

A study from 2013 even documents multiple instances of people who gained weight by exercising more.[15] Here is an excerpt from the abstract of this study: "In many interventions that are based on an exercise program intended to induce weight loss, the mean weight loss observed is modest and sometimes far less than the individual expected . . . a few actually gaining weight."

Just consider how unbelievable it is that exercising would correlate with weight gain in anyone, given the omnipresent advice to *just exercise more* to lose weight. The first reason that CICO (calories in, calories out) doesn't work is because you can't realistically move enough to affect the *calories out* number.

That is why the American Heart Association and the American College of Sports Medicine released a joint statement that said, "It is reasonable to assume that persons with relatively high daily energy expenditures would be less likely to gain weight over time, compared with those who have low energy expenditures. So far, data to support this hypothesis are not particularly compelling . . ."[16]

---

[15] https://www.ncbi.nlm.nih.gov/pmc/articles/PMC3696411

[16] https://www.ahajournals.org/doi/pdf/10.1161/circulationaha.107.185649

If we have a hypothesis about movement and weight loss that has persisted for over a century, and the data is still *not particularly compelling*, I think we have a serious error somewhere, especially considering all the time and money that has been spent on studying weight loss.

The other reason that CICO is wrong is because you can't really affect the equation by manipulating the amount of "calories in" either. You may be thinking, "Sure I can. I'll just eat less." But here is something I want you to consider: If running a mile burns a tiny amount of calories, then why would someone need 2,000 calories in a day (or whatever their total daily energy expenditure is)? It's not like we are running all day and in need of a steady stream of calories to burn. The answer is our BMR (basal metabolic rate).

We burn *most* of our calories through involuntary bodily processes like pumping blood, organ functions, and even generating body heat. Ready for the sucker punch? According to Dr. Jason Fung, "BMR may increase or decrease 30-40%. This was shown as early as 1917, when studies showed that a reduction of calorie intake by 30% is quickly met by a decrease in BMR by 30%."

Did you catch that? If you give your body less calories, it slows down your metabolism. And there is nothing you can do about it. When your body does this, the total calories you burn decreases. Simply put, if you eat five hundred fewer calories, your body will try to burn five hundred fewer calories, and it does this during processes that you have no control over. Why does your body do this? Because it wants to stay alive. A decrease in calories means that tough times may be ahead and your body needs to be extremely stingy with the energy it expends.

If you are clever, you might take this as an invitation to eat more, assuming the body will just expend more energy to burn it off (the inverse effect on BMR). Unfortunately, it doesn't work this way. There are only so many calories your accelerated BMR can dispose of before the extra calories are stored as fat (energy for later). Remember, your BMR also only rises by 30–40 percent.

This is why I promote the idea that refraining from overconsuming calories is a good thing: Not because calorie restriction is a good way to reduce your existing fat storage (BMR will just decrease), but because it reduces new fat storage. This is one of the cursed truths in this book: overeating will make you fat, but not eating enough will not make you skinny[17] (you'll just be tired and probably miserable). I know, it sucks.

This is why in 2002 the Cochran Collaboration stated that in scientific trials of calorie-restricted weight loss diets that the result was "so small as to be clinically

---

[17] https://www.ncbi.nlm.nih.gov/pmc/articles/PMC5639963

insignificant."[18] I don't know about you, but I'm not interested in killing myself by restricting my calories just so the results can be "clinically insignificant."

To summarize, "eat less, move more" doesn't work because you are almost completely helpless when it comes to changing either side of the equation. If you try to eat less, your body will force your internal processes to use less energy to compensate. If you try to move more, you will quickly realize that running a marathon every day is not a part of your life plan. So while it is technically true that our bodies obey the laws of thermodynamics, most people are unaware of BMR and the calories it uses without our deliberate choice. If you consciously controlled all the variables in the caloric equation, you could make the thermodynamics work in your favor, but as it is you are just a pawn in your own metabolism's game. So, what is the answer? I'm glad you asked.

The trick to this whole weight loss thing is realizing that everything is driven by hormones, not calories. I've been married for fifteen years, so trust me when I say, hormones drive *everything*! Your body isn't counting calories on an invisible Excel spreadsheet while you're eating and then distributing them for energy in some meticulous process throughout the day. The native language of your body is hormonal, not mathematical, and weight regulation hormones are driven by what you

---

[18] https://www.ncbi.nlm.nih.gov/pubmed/12076496

eat. If you want to lose fat, it is going to come from what you eat and the hormones your food triggers.

The first part of The Naked Code is all about the ratio of macronutrients that you consume on a daily basis. This ratio is important because it releases the correct hormones into your body and inhibits the wrong hormones so that you can burn fat while you sleep, as opposed to running twenty-three miles.

All food is comprised of three, and only three, macronutrients. They are Protein (P), Carbs (C), and Fat (F). There is lots of random information on a nutritional label, but for our purposes, most of it can be ignored. We just want to focus on the three macronutrients because this is how you size up a food in an instant and know if it will release the correct hormones in your body.

Are you ready for the first insanely powerful truth in this book? Here it is: If you eat more grams of protein than grams of fat and carbs combined in any given day, you will start to lose fat. If your protein to carb/fat ratio is greater than one, your body starts shedding fat, and it has nothing to do with exercise. This is what I mean by P > C + F. If you eat an 8-ounce rib eye steak (64 grams protein, 34 grams fat, 0 grams carbs) and 3 eggs (21 grams protein, 15 grams fat, 0 grams carbs) for breakfast, you just ate 85 grams of protein and 49 grams of carbs and fat. This is a 1.7 protein to carb and fat ratio. This meal leads to weight loss. If you keep this ratio in check throughout the day, and you do this every day, you

Nutrition Facts

Serving Size 1/2 cup (about 82g)
Servings Per Container 8

Amount Per Serving

Calories 200	Calories from Fat 130

	% Daily Value*
Total Fat 14g	**22%**
Saturated Fat 9g	45%
Trans Fat 0g	
Cholesterol 55mg	**18%**
Sodium 40mg	**2%**
Total Carbohydrate 17g	**6%**
Dietary Fiber 1g	4%
Sugars 14g	
Protein 3g	

Vitamin A 10%	•	Vitamin C 0%
Calcium 10%	•	Iron 6%

*Percent Daily Values are based on a 2,000 calorie diet. Your daily values may be higher or lower depending on your calorie needs:

		Calories:	2,000	2,500
Total Fat	Less than		65g	80g
Saturated Fat	Less than		20g	25g
Cholesterol	Less than		300mg	300 mg
Sodium	Less than		2,400mg	2,400mg
Total Carbohydrate			300g	375g
Dietary Fiber			25g	30g

Calories per gram:
Fat 9 • Carbohydrate 4 • Protein 4

will become a fat losing machine.

This food on the left (whatever the food is) will cause weight gain. Why? It only has 3 grams of protein, but it has 17 grams of carbs and 14 grams of fat. That is a 3 to 31 ratio of protein to carbs and fat, which is way less than the 1 to 1 ratio (at a minimum) we want. If this food had 28 more grams of protein, it would at least be a maintenance food (no weight gain or loss), but as it is, this food will destroy your hormones and make you fat.

This would be true even if the box said "Good source of vitamin A." Marketers want you to focus on the details that are irrelevant. That's what marketers do. Be smarter than the marketers. Rat poisoning will still kill you, even if someone puts some vitamin A in it.

A Brief History of Being Fat

The idea that carbs and fat lead to weight gain is not new. In fact, the first diet book ever written espoused a

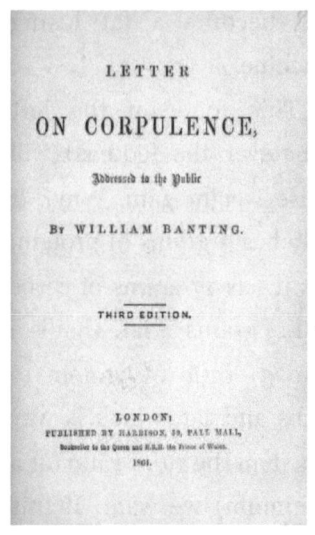

LETTER

ON CORPULENCE,

Addressed to the Public

By WILLIAM BANTING.

THIRD EDITION.

LONDON:
PUBLISHED BY HARRISON, 59, PALL MALL,
Bookseller to the Queen and H.R.H. the Prince of Wales.
1864.

very similar view in 1863.[19] William Banting was an overweight funeral director who couldn't even walk down a set of stairs facing forward because he was so large. After three decades of failed attempts to lose weight, he finally discovered how to be lean. Overjoyed, he published a booklet at personal expense, and it was massively successful. "Banting" became a synonym for "dieting." He also discovered that exercise leads to weight gain, writing, "I consulted an eminent surgeon . . . who recommended increased bodily exertion before my ordinary daily labours began, and thought rowing an excellent plan. I had the command of a good, heavy, safe boat, lived near the river, and adopted it for a couple of hours early in the morning. It is true I gained muscular vigor, but with it a prodigious appetite, which I was compelled to indulge, and consequently increased my weight, until my kind old friend advised me to forsake the exercise."

---

[19] https://archive.org/details/letteroncorpulenoobant/page/n3

Note also that the foods Banting attributed with making him fat had a terrible protein to carb and fat ratio. Banting wrote, ". . . my corpulence and subsequent obesity was not through neglect of necessary bodily activity, nor from excessive eating, drinking, or self-indulgence of any kind, except that I partook of the simple ailments of bread, milk, butter, beer, sugar, and potatoes more freely than my aged nature required . . ."

Likewise, farmers who have presumably never read Banting's booklet know exactly how to manipulate macronutrients to make their livestock fat for the slaughter. According to author John Durant, ". . . carb-heavy grains are exactly what farmers feed to livestock to fatten them up as quickly and cheaply as possible. Let me repeat that, just for good measure: grains—the base of the USDA food pyramid for humans—are what American farmers use to fatten up their livestock."[20]

Scientists have even created an obesogenic rat chow that is designed to do one thing: make rats fat for the sake of scientific studies. Guess what macronutrient ratio they landed on as optimal for their goal: low protein, high fat, and high carbs.[21]

Ever heard of *foie gras*? It's the fattened liver of a duck or goose, and it's considered a delicacy in some countries. You already know where this is going, don't

---

[20] https://www.optimize.me/quotes/john-durant/154277-yet-carb-heavy-grains-are-exactly-what-farmers-feed-to-livestock

[21] https://www.ncbi.nlm.nih.gov/pubmed/28895587

you? The way that the farmers fatten a duck liver is by feeding the duck a diet of 75 percent grains (carbs).[22]

Even gladiators knew how to get fat. Gladiators were referred to as *hordearii,* which literally means "barley men." In an attempt to find out how gladiators received this nickname, two scientists, Grossschmidt and Kanz, did an isotropic analysis on gladiator bones so that they could measure the trace minerals present in the gladiators' diets. Writing for the Archeological Institute of America, Andrew Curry said, "They turned up some surprising results. Compared to the average inhabitant of Ephesus, gladiators ate more plants and very little animal protein. The vegetarian diet had nothing to do with poverty or animal rights. Gladiators, it seems, were fat. Consuming a lot of simple carbohydrates, such as barley, and legumes, like beans, was designed for survival in the arena. Packing in the carbs also packed on the pounds." According to Grossschmidt, "Gladiators needed subcutaneous fat . . . A fat cushion protects you from cut wounds and shields nerves and blood vessels in a fight . . . a lean gladiator would have been dead meat"[23]

If you want to be a fat rat or a fat duck or a fat cow or a fat funeral director or a fat gladiator, then just follow this code: $P < C + F$, but if you want to look good naked,

---

[22] https://foiegras-factsandtruth.com/breeding/the-breeding-phase

[23] https://archive.archaeology.org/0811/abstracts/gladiator.html

follow this code: P > C + F. By simply switching the less-than symbol to a greater-than symbol you go from storing fat to burning fat.

The Science of Weight Loss

We've known, in practice, how to make things fat for years, but now we finally have the science to understand why this happens. Here are ten scientific reasons why eating more protein than fat and carbs combined leads to weight loss:

Reason 1: Fat Storage

According to Dr. Jason Fung, "Insulin is a fat-storing hormone. There's nothing wrong with that–that is simply its job. When we eat, insulin goes up, signaling the body to store some food energy as body fat . . . Higher than usual insulin levels tell our body to store more food energy as body fat."[24]

Okay, so insulin is the hormone that controls fat storage. This makes it very important that you don't become insulin resistant; if you start resisting insulin, your body responds by producing more insulin, which just signals your body to store even more fat. So the

---

[24] https://www.dietdoctor.com/my-single-best-weight-loss-tip

million-dollar question is "what makes us insulin resistant?"

According to Dr. Ted Naiman, eating fat and carbs causes insulin resistance. Dr. Naiman said, "If you want to zoom way, way out and dumb it really down, insulin resistance is from overfilled fat cells, and you overfill fat cells because you were eating carbohydrates and fat at the same time. Glucose always controls oxidation preference in your cells so that if glucose is present from the outside, you will oxidize less fat. So exogenous glucose (glucose coming in from outside) shuts off fat oxidation. If you are eating fat at the same time, it will all get stored. So if you just eat carbs and fat together, like a donut, all day, every day, you burn glucose all the time, you store fat all the time, your adipocytes fill up, bam, you've got hyperinsulinemia and insulin resistance. It's really that simple."[25]

Dr. Naiman is saying that it's the combination of eating fat and carbs that leads to being overweight. As an example, think about the hibernation of bears: They need to pack on a lot of fat that they can live off of during their months of hibernating. What do they eat leading up to their hibernation to signal for their body to start storing fat? They eat lots of berries (high carb) and lots of hazelnuts (high fat).

According to Bear.org, "The main period of weight gain in northeastern Minnesota is July and August when

---

[25] https://www.youtube.com/watch?v=JipRwP754jA&t=39s

berries and hazelnuts are abundant, making that period especially important to growth . . . Black bears are efficient berry-eaters, consuming up to 30,000 berries a day in a good year."[26]

If you plan on hibernating for a few months, you can get away with eating more carbs and fat, but our problem is that we are not bears. We live in an endless summer with endless carbs and fat, but fasting never happens. We are getting fatter year after year for no reason.

Summary: Insulin is a hormone that tells your body to store fat, and if you start eating too many carbs and fats, you will become insulin resistant. This leads to even larger quantities of the fat storage hormone being released into your body. Eat carbs and fats with low protein, and you will get fat. To crack The Naked Code, simply eat P > C + F, and you will store less fat in your body.

Reason 2: Protein Priority

Protein is so fundamental to human health that research has shown we will consume food until we meet the threshold of protein that we actually need.[27] Dr. Alison Gosby, lead author of this study and a postdoctoral fellow at the Charles Perkins Centre (University of Sydney) said, "We found that regardless of your age or

---

[26] https://bear.org/berries-a-critical-food

[27] https://www.ncbi.nlm.nih.gov/pubmed/24588967

BMI, your appetite for protein is so strong that you will keep eating until you get enough protein, which could mean you're eating much more than you should."[28]

This means that if you eat carbs and fat as the foundation of your diet, you will overconsume calories subconsciously in search of protein. However, if you start with your protein needs as the priority, as opposed to carbs and fat, your body will not have the same desire to keep eating, because it has what it needs.

Summary: We need protein, and your body knows we need protein, so you will be compelled to eat until you receive enough of it. If you consume carbs and fat as the foundation of your diet, you will overeat. However, if you consume the necessary amounts of protein as the base of your nutrition (P > C + F), you will be less likely to overeat.

Reason 3: Satiety Hormone

Ghrelin is a hormone that makes you feel hungry (remember, this whole weight loss thing is hormonal), so if you eat foods that suppress ghrelin, you will feel more satiated and eat less food. A study was conducted in 2009 to measure how different macronutrients affect the suppression of the ghrelin hormone. Their conclusion was that, "Protein induces prolonged ghrelin

---

[28] https://sydney.edu.au/news/84.html?newsstoryid=12632

suppression and is considered to be the most satiating macronutrient."[29]

Summary: A hormone called ghrelin makes us hungry, but eating a high protein diet (P > C + F) is the best way to suppress this hormone and not overeat.

Reason 4: Enter Ketosis

According to Dr. Fung, "Ketosis is a metabolic state in which your body uses fat and ketones rather than glucose (sugar) as its main fuel source . . . Ketones, or ketone bodies, are made by your liver from fat that you eat and your own body fat."

This means that if we get into a state of ketosis, we are literally using our own body fat as a fuel source, which will then reduce the amount of fat on our body.

So how do we enter ketosis? Dr. Fung continues, "Although it's possible that you may not need to be this strict, eating fewer than 20 grams of net carbs every day virtually guarantees that you'll achieve nutritional ketosis."[30]

Summary: Entering ketosis lets us reduce body fat by using it as a fuel source. The best way to enter ketosis is to eat a low-carb diet. The Naked Code, P > C + F, is a great way to enter ketosis.

---

[29] https://www.hindawi.com/journals/ijpep/2010/710852

[30] https://www.dietdoctor.com/low-carb/ketosis

Note: Some people are afraid of protein when trying to enter ketosis because of a process in our bodies called gluconeogenesis. They think that eating too much protein will lead to it being converted to sugar, which defeats the purpose of this whole way of eating. However, gluconeogenesis is demand driven, not supply driven. This means your body will convert protein to sugar if it needs to, but it won't do it just because protein is present.[31]

Reason 5: Muscle Furnaces

Remember when I said earlier that losing fat and building muscle are two almost completely different systems? This is where they overlap just a little. Protein is used to build muscle through a process called protein synthesis. The protein we ingest is broken down into amino acids and used to repair and build muscles after a workout.[32] Muscle, just by virtue of existing, burns more calories than fat. Depending on the source, a pound of muscle burns six to fifty calories a day just by being on your body.[33]

---

[31] http://www.ketotic.org/2012/08/if-you-eat-excess-protein-does-it-turn.html
http://www.tuitnutrition.com/2017/07/gluconeogenesis.html

[32] https://draxe.com/leucine

[33] https://www.verywellfit.com/how-many-calories-does-muscle-really-burn-1231074

Summary: If you eat a high protein diet, you are providing your body with the building blocks of muscle growth, and your muscle growth provides your body with a new mechanism for burning calories even when you are doing nothing. The P > C + F code will provide you with the building blocks of muscle growth and, therefore, passive calorie burning as long as you are also resistance training.

Reason 6: Quality Foods

You may have noticed that I have yet to make a list of all the forbidden foods if you want to crack The Naked Code. It may not be obvious yet, but if you follow the P > C + F code, most junk foods will break the equation, so I don't need to list them all. You end up eating quality, nutritious foods almost by accident when you follow the macronutrient ratios I recommend.

Let's say you want a Pop-Tart for breakfast because their s'more flavor is ridiculously good. Maybe you want to put them in the toaster because the warm gooeyness is worth the wait, or maybe you want to eat it cold like a maniac because you just need it now. Well, I hate to break it to you, but the choice to eat a Pop-Tart (warm or cold) will make it almost impossible to meet the goal of P > C + F during the rest of the day. If you start the morning off with six grams of protein and eighty-three grams of carbs and fat, you've dug yourself a hole that will be hard to climb out of.

Kellogg's®
Pop-Tarts®
S'mores

Nutrition Facts
Serving Size 1 Pouch (104g)

Amount Per Serving

Calories 400	Calories from Fat 90
	% Daily Value*
Total Fat 10g	**15%**
Saturated Fat 3.5g	**18%**
Trans Fat 0g	
Polyunsaturated Fat 4g	
Monounsaturated Fat 2.5g	
Cholesterol 0mg	**0%**
Sodium 420mg	**18%**
Total Carbohydrate 73g	**24%**
Dietary Fiber 1g	**5%**
Sugars 38g	
Protein 6g	

Vitamin A 0% • Vitamin C 0% • Calcium 2% • Iron 10%
Thiamin 15% • Riboflavin 10% • Niacin 10% • Folic Acid 10%

* Percent Daily Values are based on a 2,000 calorie diet. Your daily values may
be higher or lower depending on your calorie needs:

	Calories	2,000	2,500
Total Fat	Less than	65g	80g
Sat. Fat	Less than	20g	25g
Cholesterol	Less than	300mg	300mg
Sodium	Less than	2,400mg	2,400mg
Total Carbohydrate		300g	375g
Dietary Fiber		25g	30g

Ingredients: Enriched flour (wheat flour, niacin, reduced iron, vitamin B₁ [thiamin mononitrate], vitamin B₂ [riboflavin], folic acid), sugar, high fructose corn syrup, dextrose, soybean and palm oil (with TBHQ for freshness), corn syrup, whole wheat flour, bleached wheat flour, whey, contains two percent or less of: molasses, cocoa processed with alkali, cornstarch, leavening (baking soda, sodium aluminum phosphate), milk chocolate (sugar, milk, cocoa butter, chocolate), salt, modified corn starch, natural and artificial flavors, soy lecithin, gelatin, egg whites, color added, xanthan gum.
CONTAINS WHEAT, MILK, SOY AND EGG INGREDIENTS.

NLI#14978

If you ate meat the rest of the day, that would get your protein percentage up, but fat would be added to your count as well. You could slam a bunch of zero-carb, zero-fat, whey protein shakes, but you are not going to get enough calories to feel like living, and the zero-carb protein shakes taste like death. Look, I like Pop-Tarts as much as the next guy that grew up in the 80s, but they just won't work with The Naked Code.

This same line of reasoning applies to all of the other foods that will break the math. The only way to make this way of eating work is to select proteins like meat and eggs as your primary source of nutrition and add in low-sugar fruits and fibrous vegetables sparingly so as to not create an imbalance. A Pop-Tart, or anything else in a box, anything with a mascot, anything marketed to kids, anything in a bakery, or anything that tastes sweet at Starbucks, is the equivalent of launching a nuclear missile into your goals of looking good naked. You can choose s'more-flavored snacks over looking good with your shirt off. I made that decision for years. It really is your call. Just don't be delusional and think that both are possible at the same time.

This is a bottom-up approach to building a menu for yourself, as opposed to a top-down approach. A top-down approach starts with every possible food and makes a list of all the forbidden ones. This is a fool's errand because, honestly, most of what we eat should be on the banned list. Instead, let's have a bottom-up approach where we carefully select the few foods that will work and slowly build up our menu over time.

Summary: The Naked Code of P > C + F forces you to eat healthy foods because most of the junk (that will kill us) breaks the math anyway. This code also pushes us to build our menu from the bottom up with a few healthy foods.

Reason 7: Thermic Effect

Remember when I said that your basal metabolic rate is what burns most of your calories during processes like keeping your organs working. In a similar way, food has something called a "thermic effect." Different foods require different amounts of energy to break them down.

According to Dominik Pesta and Varman Samuel, "The thermic effect of food, also called diet-induced thermogenesis (DIT), is a metabolic response to food.

Food intake results in a transient increase in energy expenditure attributable to the various steps of nutrient processing (i.e. digestion, absorption, transport, metabolism and storage of nutrients). The DIT is mostly indicated as percentage increase in energy expenditure over the basic metabolic rate (BMR). DIT values are highest for protein (~15-30%), followed by CHOs (~5-10%) and fat (~0-3%)."[34]

Summary: Just by eating proteins, you'll burn one and a half to six times more calories than you will by eating carbs and at least five times more calories than eating fat. The Naked Code of P > C + F gives you an optimum thermic effect for weight loss.

Reason 8: Nonessential Carbs

Not only is protein (specifically meat protein) the priority when we consider our biological design, but carbs are universally known to be the only nonessential macronutrient. The reason carbs are nonessential is because our bodies can use protein or fat to create glucose when we need it, so we don't need to take in glucose (carbs) through our diet.[35] This is sort of like saying we don't need a green crayon because we have a

---

[34] https://www.ncbi.nlm.nih.gov/pmc/articles/PMC4258944

[35] http://www.tuitnutrition.com/2017/07/gluconeogenesis.html

blue and yellow crayon, so we can make green when we need it.

Another reason we don't need carbs is because humans do not develop any deficiencies from not consuming them. Protein is necessary (its absence will cause deficiencies), and fat is necessary (its absence will cause deficiencies), but carbs are not necessary (its absence will *not* cause deficiencies). According to an article published in *The American Journal of Clinical Nutrition*, "The usual way to discover the essentiality of nutrients is through the identification of specific deficiency syndromes. I found no evidence of a carbohydrate deficiency syndrome in humans. Protein deprivation leads to kwashiorkor, and energy deprivation leads to marasmus; however, there is no specific carbohydrate deficiency syndrome."[36]

According to Dr. Allen Last and Dr. Stephen Wilson, the SAD (Standard American Diet) is primarily carbs (50 percent) and fats (34 percent), with protein last (15 percent).[37] This means that we are eating nonessential things as a full one half of our nutrition (or malnutrition). On a similar note, over half of the American population is now diabetic or pre-diabetic.[38] If we elevate what we don't need (carbs) and decrease what

---

[36] https://academic.oup.com/ajcn/article/75/5/951/4689417

[37] https://en.wikipedia.org/wiki/
Western_pattern_diet#cite_note-7

[38] https://www.medscape.com/viewarticle/883132

we do need (protein), we should expect disastrous outcomes.

Summary: The human body does not need carbs for any reason, and we should expect poor outcomes if it is a large part of our diet. The Naked Code of P > C + F allows us to eat foods that are high in actual nutrition, instead of consuming superfluous macronutrients that lead to chronic illness.

Reason 9: Protein Micronutrients

There are thirteen vitamins and sixteen minerals (collectively known as "micronutrients") that humans need. Due to the pervasive belief that meat is worse than vegetables, the general population is completely unaware that meat is our best source of micronutrients. A protein-based diet is the best way to get the necessary micronutrients in your body, compared to eating a plant-based diet.

According to Dr. Georgia Ede, "Meat, contrary to popular belief, contains every nutrient we need in its proper form and without any anti-nutrients to interfere. Whereas plant foods all are missing certain key nutrients, and some of them are in the wrong form and harder for us to use, and they contain anti-nutrients which interfere with our ability to absorb them or utilize them."[39]

---

[39] https://www.youtube.com/watch?v=UR7H9xeMYME&t=1255s

As an example, consider the micronutrient comparison between ground beef and spinach. Surprisingly, beef actually provides more micronutrients than even spinach does.[40]

Vegetarians actually have to be very concerned with their micronutrient deficiencies. Writing in *Psychology Today*, Dr. Georgia Ede goes on to say, "The brain-healthy nutrients that plant-eaters in developed countries need to be the most concerned about are: DHA, vitamin B12, vitamin K2 (MK-4), zinc, iron, riboflavin, and vitamin D3. It is common knowledge that vegan diets need to be supplemented with B12, but many people are under the impression that colorful fruits and vegetables are excellent sources of most other vital nutrients. I practice at Smith College, where 4% of my students eat a vegan diet—that is twice the national average compared to other college campuses; the great majority of them cite compassion for animals or environmental concerns—not health—as their primary motivation. Many of the students I treat who choose a vegan diet only supplement B12, and some don't take any supplements at all. The science is clear on this point: unsupplemented vegan diets pose great danger to brain health."[41]

---

[40] https://paleoleap.com/meat-protein

[41] https://www.psychologytoday.com/intl/blog/diagnosis-diet/201709/the-vegan-brain

Summary: Humans need micronutrients (vitamins and minerals), but few people realize that a protein-based diet is the best way to get those micronutrients. If you follow The Naked Code of P > C + F, you will be on the right track to fulfill your micronutrient needs.

Reason 10: Build or Energize

Our bodies view carbs and fat as energy, but they view protein as the building blocks to repair our bodies and build muscle. When we eat a high-carb and high-fat diet, we are taking in the energy necessary to go on an epic journey. Are we climbing Everest? Are we hiking in the Sahara? Nope, we're just watching *Stranger Things* on Netflix, again. The problem is that now we have this surplus of energy, and our bodies are extremely frugal. Your body decides to store this extra energy for later in its fat backpack.

If you can view carbs and fat as pure energy—energy that will be stored as fat—it will give you the right mindset toward your food. If you are swimming the English Channel, then sure, have a sweet potato. Otherwise, I'd recommend the rotisserie chicken. The Standard American Diet consists of enough energy to fly to the moon and back, but we're just hanging out on the couch.

If you eat a low-carb diet along with the appropriate amount of fat, you might be worried about running out of energy, but remember, protein can become energy through gluconeogenesis. However, carbs and fat cannot become all the essential amino acids in protein. David Harrison at Rosalind Franklin University of Medicine and Science said, "Without all of the essential amino acids being present in the diet, it is not possible to build body proteins from these non-essential amino acids. Importantly, the fatty acids from fats cannot contribute to the production of amino acids or proteins."[42] By eating protein you are eating the macronutrient that can build when necessary and energize when it must, and it is only stored as fat in some situations.

The idea that protein consumption doesn't easily lead to fat storage is an incredibly important point to consider. In 2017, researchers wanted to know what would happen if you fed someone too many calories of different macronutrients. After surveying all the relevant literature, their findings are astounding. They said, ". . . recent evidence suggests that there is a quantitative difference in protein versus carbohydrate and/or fat overfeeding as it relates to body composition. Protein overfeeding or the consumption of a high protein diet may not result in a gain in body weight or fat mass despite consuming calories that exceed one's normal or habitual intake . . . In conclusion, it is evident that overfeeding on carbohydrate and/or fat results in body composition alterations that are different than

---

[42] https://www.quora.com/Can-fats-be-converted-into-protein/answer/David-Harrison-90

overfeeding on protein. It is commonly believed that 3,500 kcal is equivalent to 0.45 kg (1 pound) of fat and that changing energy balance in accordance with this will produce predictable changes in body weight. However, the overfeeding literature to date does not support this assertion. Dietary protein appears to have a protective effect against fat gain during times of energy surplus, especially when combined with resistance training. Therefore, the evidence suggests that dietary protein may be the key macronutrient in terms of promoting positive changes in body composition."[43]

Summary: All food is either for building or energizing. If we eat primarily carbs and fat (energy) instead of protein (building), then we are preparing for a massive energy expenditure that never happens, and our frugal bodies store the hard-won energy as fat. However, protein can serve both functions as needed and rarely becomes fat. If you eat in order to crack The Naked Code, $P > C + F$, you will have the proper energy for your actual activities, without the extra fat.

The Essence of the Scientific Argument

There is not one scientific reason why this code works to make you look good naked, there are at least ten reasons.

---

43 https://www.ncbi.nlm.nih.gov/pmc/articles/PMC5786199

When you eat a diet higher in protein than carbs and fat the following occurs:

- You lower your insulin and store less fat.

- You eat fewer calories since you naturally prioritize your protein intake.

- You suppress your hunger hormones with high protein consumption, so you feel satiated.

- You enter ketosis, which allows you to burn your body fat as a fuel source for energy.

- You eat nutritious foods by default since processed junk foods have the wrong ratio of macronutrients.

- You eat the foods that have the largest impact on increasing your metabolism.

- You avoid most carbohydrates, the nonessential macronutrient that serves no vital purpose in your body.

- You have more of the micronutrient vitamins and minerals that you need to be healthy.

- Your primary source of food is not stored as fat for future energy expenditure.

The Carnivore Movement

As people have discovered the effectiveness of eating more protein than carbs and fat, it has given rise to an entire carnivore movement. Meat is the superfood of The Naked Code because it is mostly protein and healthy fat with zero carbohydrates. This has led to a growing number of people who eat meat as their primary, or even only, source of food. The carnivores seem to be thriving for all of the reasons mentioned in this chapter. There are a few different varieties of the modern day carnivore diet:

- **Keto Carnivore**: This diet is a meat-based spin-off of the popular keto diet. Keto carnivores eat meat as their primary food, but they will still consume some of the typical keto foods; These include dairy, some types of nuts, low-carb vegetables (i.e. broccoli or asparagus), and low-sugar fruits (i.e. blackberries and blueberries). A traditional keto diet is very low in carbs, but it is also high in fats. This is what makes keto carnivores different. Most keto carnivores would consume a macronutrient ratio that would fit within The Naked Code protocol of P > C + F, but the same is not true for followers of a traditional keto diet.

- **Relaxed Carnivore**: This diet consists primarily of meat and animal by-products, like eggs and dairy. Relaxed carnivores may also consume herbs, spices, honey, and even coffee or tea. Unlike the keto carnivores, this group doesn't eat any vegetables or fruit. A relaxed carnivore would most likely eat a diet that follows The Naked Code of P > C + F.

- **Strict Carnivore**: This diet consists of meat, organs, water, and salt. People who follow a strict carnivore diet don't consume animal by-products like dairy or eggs, they don't cook with herbs and spices, and they don't drink coffee or tea. Some people with serious health issues are finding incredible success with this way of eating. Mikhaila Peterson, one of the most popular influencers in favor of a strict carnivore diet said, "The food pyramid is a lie, meat fat is good for you, and many (if not most) health problems are treatable with diet alone. I'm in remission from severe arthritis (multiple joints replaced), chronic fatigue, depression and a plethora of other symptoms from changing how I eat." Strict carnivores eat a macronutrient ratio that easily follows The Naked Code of P > C + F.

Since keto carnivore is the easiest way to begin eating more protein than carbs and fat, the rest of this book will guide you toward that way of eating. I currently eat a keto carnivore or a relaxed carnivore diet on most days. Sometimes I will have a strict carnivore day, but this only works when I am away from my family. Keto carnivore is easier when I am feeding my kids because they enjoy having a vegetable side dish to go with their chicken breast or steak.

Increasing Your Fat Intake

As you reach your ideal body fat percentage you should start eating more dietary fat. When you eat more protein than carbs and fat then your body is using your stored body fat as energy. This is exactly what we want to happen, but once you reach your optimal body composition you should start increasing your dietary fat intake so that you have enough energy. You don't want your body to breakdown your muscle protein for energy.

The vast majority of the population has enough stored body fat to live for many weeks without thinking about their dietary fat intake, but this might not be the case after you reach your goal. Once you achieve your ideal body composition, continue to keep your carb intake very low, but experiment with your fat to protein ratio to find the balance that works for you. Increase your fat intake by eating fattier cuts of meat or by cooking in more beef tallow. Don't increase your fat intake by eating ultra-processed foods. Carbs are the true villain of this book, not fat. Humans need fat to live.

Frequently Asked Questions

Protein and meat have been vilified for so long that there are predictable questions that come up whenever I talk about this way of eating. I am going to do a rapid-fire Q & A session to address the biggest questions, and I'll include resources for further investigation with each answer.

Q: Does eating too much meat cause cancer?

A: No. In fact, if you read Vilhjalmur Stefansson's book, *Cancer: Disease of Civilization?,* he studied the Inuit people, whose diet consisted of 90 percent meat and fish and for who six to nine months at a time would go with no carbohydrates at all, and they didn't have a single instance of cancer until they adopted a Western way of eating.[44]

---

[44] http://solus.life/stefansson

Q: If I eat too much protein, will it get converted to fat?

A: No. A study was done where three groups were all overfed calories for eight weeks. Group one had a low-protein diet, group two had a medium-protein diet, and group three had a high-protein diet. All groups gained weight by being overfed, but this was the conclusion: "Among persons living in a controlled setting, calories alone account for the increase in fat; protein affected energy expenditure and storage of lean body mass, but not body fat storage." The low-protein group gained the least weight, but what they did gain was mostly fat. The high-protein group had the highest lean body mass after the study. Overeating protein will increase your weight via lean body mass, but it will not increase your fat like the other micronutrients will.[45]

Q: If I eat this much meat, will I be constipated since I won't get enough fiber?

A: No. The need for fiber is one of the great hoaxes of our era. There was a study that used a high-fiber diet to treat IBS (irritable bowel syndrome), and they discovered that fiber was part of the problem. They stated in the conclusion, "Indeed, in some cases, insoluble fibers may worsen the clinical outcome."[46] A second study wanted

[45] https://www.ncbi.nlm.nih.gov/pubmed/22215165

[46] https://www.ncbi.nlm.nih.gov/pubmed/14984370

to see what happens if you lower the fiber in the diets of constipated patients. They said, "Idiopathic constipation and its associated symptoms can be effectively reduced by stopping or even lowering the intake of dietary fiber."[47] This is the exact opposite of what everyone expects. A third study aimed at discovering if fiber helped patients with diverticulosis (pockets in the colon that cause bloating and constipation) concluded by saying, "A high-fiber diet and increased frequency of bowel movements are associated with greater, rather than lower, prevalence of diverticulosis."[48] The truth is that fiber will mess you up, and you don't need it.

Q: Isn't meat high in saturated fat, which causes cholesterol and heart diseases?

A: No. The sugar industry knew about links to coronary heart disease and sugar in the 1950s, so they sponsored a study that downplayed the role of sugar and shifted the blame to meat. The Sugar Research Foundation (the sugar industry) was involved in the production of this paper at every step.[49]

Ancel Keys, a scientist in the 1950s, also popularized the idea that consuming meat leads to heart disease by

---

[47] https://www.ncbi.nlm.nih.gov/pmc/articles/PMC3435786

[48] https://www.ncbi.nlm.nih.gov/pubmed/22062360

[49] https://jamanetwork.com/journals/jamainternalmedicine/article-abstract/2548255

saying, "an excess of saturated fats in the diet, from red meat, cheese, butter, and eggs, raises cholesterol, which congeals on the inside of coronary arteries, causing them to harden and narrow, until the flow of blood is staunched and the heart seizes up." This statement was based off of his Seven Countries Study, which we now know was a complete sham. *The Guardian* reported on the study, saying, "Despite its monumental stature, however, the Seven Countries Study, which was the basis for a cascade of subsequent papers by its original authors, was a rickety construction. There was no objective basis for the countries chosen by Keys, and it is hard to avoid the conclusion that he picked only those he suspected would support his hypothesis." He cherry-picked the data to fit the conclusion he needed, not the other way around.[50]

I recommend reading *The Cholesterol Myths*, by Dr. Uffe Ravnskov to study this topic further.[51]

---

[50] https://www.theguardian.com/society/2016/apr/07/the-sugar-conspiracy-robert-lustig-john-yudkin

[51] http://www.ravnskov.nu/cm

Q: Will eating this much protein harm my kidneys?

A: No. A study was done where two men ate nothing but meat for an entire year, just to see the effects on kidney function, and they showed no adverse reactions.[52]

In 2016, another study published in the *Journal of Nutrition and Metabolism* did a randomized study with fourteen men to see the effects of year-long high-protein diet. The scientists concluded, "Our investigation discovered that, in resistance-trained men that consumed a high protein diet (~2.51–3.32 g/kg/d) for one year, there were no harmful effects on measures of blood lipids as well as liver and kidney function. In addition, despite the total increase in energy intake during the high protein phase, subjects did not experience an increase in fat mass."[53]

Q: Will eating this much meat give me scurvy?

A: No. According to *The American Journal of Digestive Diseases*, "Meat exclusive of such visceral organ as the liver has been regarded as a food playing no role or at least a very insignificant role as an antiscorbutic. The inability of muscle meat to prevent and to cure scurvy is an idea which has taken root because of the experiments

---

[52] https://justmeat.co/docs/prolonged-meat-diets-walter-s-mclellan-eugen-f-du-bois.pdf

[53] https://www.hindawi.com/journals/jnme/2016/9104792

of the earlier investigators. These workers did not appreciate the importance of freshly killed meat in contradistinction to fresh market meat. Furthermore, they used the guinea pig as a test animal. This animal has a limited gastrointestinal capacity. It can, therefore, be fed only a small quantity of a food biologically assayed for vitamin C content. If this small quantity possessed sufficient vitamin C to cure or prevent scurvy, the food was said to possess antiscorbutic potency. If, however, this small quantity did not contain sufficient vitamin C to cure or prevent scurvy, the food was regarded as one devoid of antiscorbutic potency. More recent experiments with freshly killed meat indicate that quantities fed within the physical capacity of the guinea pig possessed decided antiscorbutic value. The chemical method for vitamin C does not have the disadvantages of the guinea pig bio-assay method."[54]

This means that early studies that seemed to show that meat didn't have enough vitamin C to cure scurvy were actually erroneous due to the biology of the guinea pig, and later studies show that meat can cure scurvy.

I would recommend watching Amber O'Hearn's presentation at Carnivore Con for further study. It is titled "Rethinking RDAs (Recommended Daily Allowances)"[55]

---

[54] https://link.springer.com/article/10.1007/BF03014680

[55] https://www.youtube.com/watch?v=kX4qsJd_Plc

CHAPTER 2

RETHINKING YOUR MEALS

My Typical Meals

For some people, the last chapter on the science of macronutrient ratios was boring and painful to read, and for others it will be your favorite part of this book. However, it's important that you know *why* before you learn *how*. If you are not fully convinced on the science, then you will give up when adversity hits.

Now, let me walk you through a typical day of my eating schedule, so we can make this practical. Remember, we are not going for insane variety with our personal menu of food. We are starting simple and building off of staples. Also, none of the food I make is complicated or uses very many ingredients or even looks that good. There will be no beautiful cookbook-style images of what I'm eating. I eat food, not art. For breakfast, I have a few different possibilities:

Breakfast Option 1

I skip breakfast. I'm a fan of intermittent fasting, and I honestly don't feel very hungry when I wake up. The only times I find myself wanting a large breakfast are if I didn't get enough protein the day before.

Breakfast Option 2

I have four to six shots of espresso with heavy cream and nothing else. This gives me some fat, almost no carbs, and no protein. This is a simple way for me to get some caffeine into my system without spending much time on prep. It doesn't get me into a huge protein deficit to start the day (just a small deficit). I've learned that getting too many carbs and fat at the start the day usually means I won't get the ratios I'm looking for by the end of the day.

Breakfast Option 3

I drink a protein shake and nothing else. I try to get a couple scoops of whey protein in about eight ounces of water, which (depending on the brand) will get me about forty grams of protein and about seven grams of carbs (if I opt for the flavored stuff, which I usually do). This gives me a massive jump-start on hitting my macro ratios for the day.

Breakfast Option 4

I have a couple eggs and a small steak. This would be considered a large breakfast for me. The steak and eggs both have the protein to carb and fat ratio that I'm looking for, so this meal puts me on track for the day. I call foods like steak and eggs "Naked Foods" because the correct ratio is present in the individual food itself. So if you ate nothing but Naked Foods, you would automatically hit the P > C + F goal.

For lunch, I usually opt to have the same thing every day . . . nothing. If I chose option 2, 3, or 4, for breakfast, by lunchtime I'm just not even close to being ready to eat. Having almost any calories when I wake up feels like jet fuel for the first part of the day. If I fasted for breakfast, I might want something to eat by two p.m. for a late lunch. If so, my go-to option for lunch is Pollo Tropical. I get two chicken breasts and cilantro sauce, and this gives me a massive bump in protein with very few carbs and fat. Side note: this lunch is ridiculously good.

For dinner, I usually base everything around a chunk of protein. I'm not going to explain my thought process behind each meal because I really just select something that sounds good, as long as I get a lot of protein and not too many carbs and fat:

Dinner Option 1

Rib eye and asparagus spears

Dinner Option 2

Bun-less burger with cheddar cheese and mayonnaise, and a side of broccoli

Dinner Option 3

Chicken breast and brussels sprouts

Dinner Option 4

Pulled pork with low-carb BBQ sauce and mashed cauliflower

Dinner Option 5

Fish and mixed vegetables

Dinner Option 6

Pork chops with low-carb BBQ sauce and a Caesar salad

Dinner Option 7

Meatballs and low-carb pasta sauce

You get the idea. It's really not complicated. Simply select a meat and add a side of something that isn't a nutritional disaster. The meat usually has an amazing ratio, and the sides usually have a less than desirable ratio, but it works out in the end for our goals. Some of my dinner meals by themselves will have a few too many carbs or too much fat, but don't forget to add my breakfast and lunch to the equation. If I had a protein shake or eggs and steak for breakfast or if I had a chicken breast for lunch, I am way ahead on my protein goals before going into dinner. Also, I drop the sides if I'm eating alone. I usually only cook sides if we are having a family meal.

How to Hunt and Cook Your Meat

If you are going to crack The Naked Code, I would recommend investing in a decent grill. I almost never grilled out before my journey into being healthy. Everything was in a box, so there wasn't much of a need for a grill. Now, I fire up the grill all the time without even thinking about it. I even bought two propane tanks so I never run out. Cooking on a grill is better than cooking on a stove because it is easier to clean up, and the food tastes better.

I would also suggest investing in a cast iron skillet that you can fit in the grill when the top is closed. This is where you put any vegetables so they can be cooking while the meat is being grilled. They make cast iron skillets with a removable rubber grip for transporting it while it's hot. You'll want this type to get the vegetables into the house easily.

Spices are also super important. Chicken by itself is, well, kind of bland, but if you flavor it with McCormick Perfect Pinch Rotisserie Chicken Seasoning (my personal favorite), it will explode with flavor. Spices can also be used generously on beef, pork, and more, not just chicken. Spices are usually much better than sauces in terms of not screwing up your macros, so experiment with spices until you find the ones that work for you.

It also becomes important to know where your local butcher shop is and to make a habit of stopping by there on a regular basis. With how much protein you are going to be eating, you'll need a steady supply of fresh meat. The meat will be higher quality and the price will probably be better if you shop at a local butcher, as opposed to other sources. I just landed in Costa Rica where I'll be staying with my family for a couple months, and on my second day here I found the local butcher. With no cell signal and no Google Maps, I wandered around a busy city square in Latin America until I saw a storefront of epic protein goodness. Then I used my non-existent Spanish to order three kilos of fresh meat.

When people hear about all the fresh meat I eat in my diet, they assume that my grocery bill is astronomically high. In reality, I probably spend less than I did before. Yes, I eat better cuts of meat, but I'm not filling my cart with massive amounts of boxed foods that disappear almost instantly because I overeat them. I'm also not eating many fruits (what I refer to as *wet candy*), so this saves me money. Eating a high-protein diet even makes intermittent fasting easy, so I usually skip at least one meal a day, which saves money.

Another often overlooked financial aspect to this way of eating is the money you can save by eliminating medications. My dad was able to stop taking his insulin shots, among other medications, which saved him over 300 dollars a month. Just imagine all the future medications that this way of eating will also prevent him from needing and buying.

Some people are concerned with how to eat out while following The Naked Code. Maybe you have a busy schedule, or travel for work, or just hate cooking. Whatever the reason, eating out is actually really easy to do. Just order a piece of meat, tell them to hold the bread, and then select a side that isn't stupid. In my experience, it's possible to create a great meal at 80 percent of the restaurants you'll visit. Pizza places usually have wings. Pasta restaurants usually have a cut of chicken. Steak houses usually have . . . well . . . steak. Fast food joints usually have bun-less burgers.

Ready for a fast food hack that can save you tons of money? Sadly, it took me a long time to learn this one.

Don't order the regular burger without the bun. Just order the number of patties you want with the number of cheese slices you want. Instead of paying for the regularly priced burger, they will sometimes only charge you for the price of the patties and cheese, which is usually far less. This won't work everywhere, but it will work at some restaurants, so it's worth asking.

The Perfect Naked Foods

If this is your first time thinking about which macronutrients are in your food, you might find it difficult to know which foods are good and which foods are bad for this way of eating. The best method I've found is to use the MyFitnessPal app. You can search for any food on this app, whether from a grocery store or a restaurant, and it will tell you what the macronutrient breakdown is. You can even use the app to track your meals every day so that you can ensure you achieve the goal of P > C + F.

Naked Foods are the foods that have the correct ratio of macronutrients built into the food itself. For instance, an egg is a perfect Naked Food because it has seven grams of protein and five grams of fat, with zero carbs. You know, without even thinking about it, that eggs are a food that will always get you closer to your goal. Below is a list of my favorite Naked Foods along with their approximate protein to carb and fat ratio information.

Food	Protein Grams	Carbs Grams	Fat Grams	Ratio Grams
Protein Powder 1 scoop	20	3	0	20:3
Eggs 1 egg	7	0	5	7:5
Ground Beef 1 ounce	7	0	6	7:6
Rib eye 1 ounce	6	0	5.5	12:11
Chicken Breast 1 ounce	6	0	1	6:1
Tilapia 1 ounce	2	0	0	2:0
Salmon 1 ounce	5	0	3	5:3
Yellowtail Sashimi 1 ounce	7	0	2	7:2
Sausage Link 1 link	6	0	4	3:2
Pulled Pork 1 ounce	6	0	3	2:1
Pork Chop 1 chop	13	0	4	13:4
Pork Rinds 1 ounce	8	0	5	8:5

Sliced Ham 1 ounce	7	0	1	7:1
Cottage Cheese 1 ounce	2	1	0	2:1
Plain Greek Yogurt 1 ounce	2	1	0	2:1

There are a lot of other Naked Foods, but these are just some of my favorite options. If you start your day with a protein shake, eat a chicken breast or fish at some point as your main protein, and mix in high-fiber, low-starch vegetables sparingly, you will lose your excess fat.

Drinks and Cooking Oils

After people realize how they should think about their main dishes and side dishes then they usually start asking about things like drinks and cooking oils. What we choose to drink throughout the day, and what we cook our food in, can have a large impact on our body composition and general health.

Our drinks should follow The Naked Code. Don't drink anything that has more grams of fat and carbs than protein. Drinks don't usually have any protein, so your only options are really unsweetened coffee, unsweetened tea, water, and zero calorie drinks. Water is the absolute best choice for anyone wanting to look good naked. It's worth noting that the artificial sweeteners like those found in Diet Coke, Coke Zero, Powerade Zero, and most other zero calorie drinks that are sweet, do have an impact on our insulin levels, and therefore could impact our fat loss.

Now that you are cooking a lot of meat it's important that you choose the right oils and fats to cook in. Avoid vegetable oils and seed oils like soybean oil, canola oil, corn oil, cottonseed oil, sunflower oil, peanut oil, sesame oil, and rice bran oil, as the ratio of omega-6 fatty acids compared to omega-3 fatty acids is very high, which has been associated with "chronic inflammatory diseases such as nonalcoholic fatty liver disease (NAFLD), cardiovascular disease, obesity, inflammatory bowel disease (IBD), rheumatoid arthritis, and Alzheimer's disease (AD)."[56] I would recommend cooking in beef tallow, coconut oil, avocado oil, or extra virgin olive oil. Coconuts, avocados, and olives, can all three be classified as fruits (so not a vegetable oil).

Addiction and Flu-Like Symptoms

Most people are addicted to carbs, whether they will admit it or not. I used to say I was a carb-oholic! I don't

---

[56] https://www.ncbi.nlm.nih.gov/pubmed/22570770

think the word addiction is too strong since carbohydrates are nonessential for life, overconsuming them is linked with chronic diseases, and we experience negative withdrawal symptoms for some period of time when we abstain from them, yet we don't want to live life without them. Sounds like an addiction to me.

It's important that you see carbs as a drug so that when you go through an unpleasant period of withdrawal, you won't assume that the low-carb way of eating is bad for you. This would be like someone using cocaine because every time they try to stop, it feels bad.

Honestly, you might feel terrible for the first few weeks as your body transitions to this new way of eating. Some people describe the feeling as flu-like. Your body is going through a metamorphosis as it learns how to do the one thing that it never had to do: burn your fat as energy. With a steady stream of carbs, your body was always topped off with a readily available energy supply from your diet, so it burned what carbs it could as energy, then stored the rest of the carbs and fat in your diet as body fat. Now, you are forcing your body to use your stored body fat as energy since you've removed the ready supply of carbs.

Your body actually prefers to burn fat for fuel, but there is still a transition period. Once you get through the transition, you will know why your body prefers its new fuel source (body fat). You will have elevated energy. You won't have that crash in the middle of the day when it's hard to stay awake. You will have clarity of mind and be able to focus unusually well. You will stop obsessing about your next meal since your blood sugar levels are not rising and falling all the time. A lot of people prone to depression even report being less depressed, or not depressed at all, on a lower-carb diet. In fact, a low-carb diet is even used to treat epilepsy. We are designed to run on body fat, not just a steady stream of carbs.

As you eat fewer carbs, you are going to lose a lot of the sodium in your body. I would highly recommend salting your food generously at every meal because when your body gets low on electrolytes (like salt), your energy can plummet, and you will feel terrible. Eating more salt is a quick and easy fix to some of these transition symptoms.

People with high blood pressure may have learned to fear salt, but the truth is that having too little salt is what is actually dangerous. According to the Institute of Medicine, "Existing evidence, however, does not support either a positive or negative effect of lowering sodium intake to <2300 mg/d in terms of cardiovascular risk or mortality in the general population." However, in regards to heart failure the committee said, "The committee concluded that there is sufficient evidence to suggest a negative effect of low sodium intakes." Dr. Fung, commentating on these findings, said, "The very patients we were most strenuously recommending to reduce their salt would be harmed the most."[57]

Insights on Weight Loss

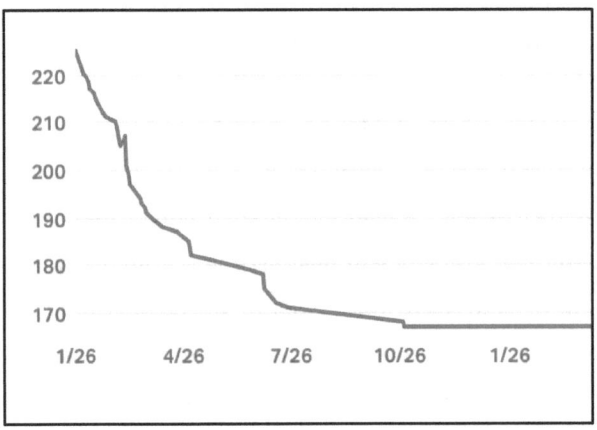

Above is my actual weight loss chart (I tracked everything in MyFitnessPal). I went from 225 pounds to 167 pounds in about nine months. During this incredible journey, I discovered some surprising things about weight loss that I want to pass on.

First, if you are losing more than a couple pounds a week, you are not just losing fat, it's also water weight. Your body can only use so much fat for energy. I lost an average of .2 pounds a day (or 1.4 pounds a week). You

---

[57] https://medium.com/@drjasonfung/the-salt-scam-1973d73dccd

need to have realistic expectations for how long it will take you to reach your goals.

Second, weight loss is not linear. I gained weight on some days, and I have no idea why. Don't get discouraged with weird blips in your progress.

Third, your weight loss will slow down as you reach your optimal body weight. The closer you get to your goal, the slower you'll see movement. It was obvious to me when it was time to start building muscle because my body had found a natural homeostasis, and I was no longer losing weight, nor did I want to.

What should you do if you stop losing weight for longer than two weeks and you haven't reached your goal weight? This is called "hitting a plateau." The first thing I would do is look at my daily calorie intake. Remember, this isn't because a calorie decrease causes weight loss (your BMI just slows down), but because a calorie surplus will cause weight gain. Most people are so out of touch with their body that they actually require far fewer calories than they think.

To ensure you don't overeat, you must develop a healthy relationship with hunger. Being full is not the goal of a meal, as this will lead to weight gain. Satiety is the goal, not fullness. It's also important to know that hunger is a feeling that comes and goes quite quickly. I have fasted for three days before, and for the majority of that time, I didn't feel hungry. Just because you have a slight desire to eat does not mean you need to react.

Thousands of years ago hunger pangs wouldn't be satisfied until hours or days later when prey had been hunted and prepared. Hunger is merely a very early alert to start the process of finding food. Hunger is not a red alert siren to immediately eat. Otherwise, hunger would have been a useless signal for most of our past.

No one can tell you the number of calories you should eat to not gain weight. Everyone's biology is unique enough that you will have to experiment with yourself. When I type my data into an online calorie calculator, it recommends 2,500 calories to maintain my current weight. I know from personal experience that this is far too many calories. 1,750 calories is closer to my actual maintenance needs. Until I hit my homeostasis goal weight, I knew if I ate about 1,750 calories and ate mostly protein, some fat, and very few carbs, that I would lose weight almost every day.

A weight loss question I often get is, "Will I have to eat this way forever to keep my weight loss results?" My response is usually, "You are free to go back to the Standard American Diet (SAD) whenever you want, and you can keep the results of the Standard American Diet that come along with that decision. It's your choice."

Really, this is an odd question if you think about it. It's like wanting an award for losing. If you make bad choices, you will get bad outcomes, and at no point are you free to make bad decisions without consequences. You will not get a weight loss medal for coming in last place because you chose to eat a Standard American Diet. Sorry.

Here's another way to think about it: If someone was eating poison everyday and they felt miserable, I would point out to them that they should probably stop ingesting poison. Let's say they went away, took my advice, and started feeling great. Then imagine that they came back concerned, asking, "Will I have to avoid poison forever to keep these positive results?" Um, what?!

The great thing about The Naked Code is that it is a lifelong eating plan, not a quick fix. Once you get over the transition phase, you will want to eat this way.

The Naked Code

CHAPTER 3

THE SIMPLE SCIENCE OF GAINING MUSCLE

The Anatomy of a Muscle

Have you ever been asked if you prefer dark meat or white meat when ordering chicken? Some people prefer the taste of one over the other. These two colors of meat actually represent the different kinds of muscles in many animals. Red (dark) muscles are red because of the amount of myoglobin (a red pigment) found in those muscles.

It's important to note that these two kinds of muscle don't just differ in color, they also differ in function. According to Juleen Zierath and John Hawley, "The

French anatomist Louis Antoine Ranvier had already observed that some muscles of the rabbit were redder in color, and contracted in a slower, more sustained manner, than paler muscles of the same animal."[58]

Red muscles contract more slowly, and white muscles contract more quickly. This is why you will often hear these muscles referred to as fast-twitch muscles or slow-twitch muscles. It's also important to realize that these slow and fast muscle fibers are interspersed throughout a single muscle in humans. We don't just have red muscles or white muscles. Our muscles are much more mixed than the muscles of a chicken.

In the scientific literature, slow-twitch muscle fibers are also called type 1 muscle fibers, and fast-twitch muscle fibers are also called type 2 muscle fibers. In addition to contracting slower, type 2 muscles also fatigue more quickly.[59]

Then, just to make things a bit more complicated, type 2 muscles are further subdivided into three categories: type 2A, type 2B, and type 2X. The main difference in type 2A and type 2B/2X is that type 2A is oxidative, while type 2B/2X is glycolytic. This is important because there is an inverse relationship to the size of muscle fibers and their oxidative ability.[60]

---

[58] https://www.ncbi.nlm.nih.gov/pmc/articles/PMC521732/#pbio-0020348

[59] https://www.ncbi.nlm.nih.gov/m/pubmed/6462127

[60] https://www.ncbi.nlm.nih.gov/pmc/articles/PMC2957584

I know that is a lot of jargon, so here is a simple table to keep all of this information about muscle fibers straight:

	Type 1	Type 2A	Type 2B	Type 2X
Color	Red	White	White	White
Speed	Slow	Fast	Fast	Fast
Fatigue	Slowly	Quickly	Quickly	Quickly
Metabolism	Oxidative	Oxidative	Glycolytic	Glycolytic
Size	Small	Small	Large	Large

Why does any of this matter? If our goal is to look good naked, then we are interested in type 2B and type 2X muscle fibers. These are the fibers that decide the size and shape of the muscles on our body (they are the largest fibers). If we understand how type 2B and type 2X muscle fibers work, we can grow our muscles.

So, how do we get muscle fibers to grow? Despite popular opinion, muscles don't grow during exercise; they actually grow as a response to the stimulus of exercise. Sure, your muscles get bigger during a workout, but this is blood filling your muscles (what is commonly called a "pump"). This is not the growth of actual muscle tissue, which is why the swelling goes down after a few hours. As Christian Finn, an expert on building muscle, said, "Getting a pump, in and of itself, isn't essential for muscle growth. It is possible to build muscle without a pump. What's more, if you don't get a pump, it doesn't necessarily mean you're doing anything wrong."[61]

Therefore, we are interested in the actual growth of muscle cells, also called "hypertrophy," not the blood-filling process, also called a "pump." It's during hypertrophy that true muscle growth happens. So the next question is, how do we initiate hypertrophy in our type 2B and type 2X muscle tissue?

The important stimulus for creating real growth in your muscles is fatigue. According to Chris Beardsley, the expert who literally wrote the book on hypertrophy, "As we fatigue, the shortening speed of the muscle fibers reduces and motor unit recruitment increases. These are the key factors that are required for stimulating hypertrophy, because they allow high-threshold motor units to experience sufficiently high levels of mechanical loading."[62]

This means we need to fatigue our type 2B and type 2X muscle fibers to get them to grow, but this creates a problem. The body doesn't recruit these muscle fibers unless they are absolutely necessary for the task at hand. According to Pete McCall, "Fast-twitch fibers have a high threshold and will be recruited or activated only when

---

[61] https://muscleevo.net/pump-muscle

[62] https://medium.com/@SandCResearch/how-does-proximity-to-failure-affect-hypertrophy-e39653d41e96

the force demands are greater than the slow-twitch fibers can meet . . . Fast-twitch fibers can generate more force, but are quicker to fatigue when compared to slow-twitch fibers."[63]

Basically, slow-twitch muscle fibers are used during our everyday tasks like walking, cooking, and playing with our kids. During these kinds of activities, our type 2 muscle fibers are not activated; they are not fatigued, and therefore they do not experience hypertrophy and growth. Being active doesn't make your muscles grow. The only way to get your muscles to grow is to deeply fatigue them to the point that your type 1 fibers can't handle the stimulus, your type 2 fibers are recruited, and then they are also fatigued.

If you are engaged in an activity for more than a minute or two, it is safe to say that you are utilizing type 1 muscle fibers. Type 2 fibers fatigue much quicker than this. The best way to activate and fatigue 2B and 2X fibers is through some kind of exercise that requires generating extreme force for a short amount of time, since that's what these fibers were designed for. This leads us to the importance of resistance training.

---

[63] https://www.acefitness.org/education-and-resources/professional/expert-articles/5714/muscle-fiber-types-fast-twitch-vs-slow-twitch

The Dominance of Resistance Training

In regard to muscle fatigue in type 2B and 2X fibers and the subsequent muscle growth, there is a time-tested method that towers above all alternatives as the de facto standard: resistance training. Resistance training is the act of moving heavy weight that resists against your muscles. It's a simple concept, but the results have been marveled at for thousands of years.

About 2,500 years ago, Milo of Croton, dominated the Olympic Games in Greece. He won the men's wrestling category five years in a row in the Olympics, along with winning the same category at the Pythian Games seven times, at the Isthmian Games ten times, and at the Nemean Games nine times, making him a grand slam winner (Periodonikes) five times. So how did he develop his superhuman strength? He used primitive resistance training.

The story of Milo's strength begins with a calf that was born near Milo's home. He decided to pick up the calf and carry it home (presumably to strengthen his muscles), and he continued this habit every day. Since the calf was naturally getting heavier every day, Milo was engaged in progressive resistance training by accident. Not only was he lifting heavy weights, but the poundage was also ever-increasing. He was enduring muscle fatigue through this resistance, and he grew bigger and stronger every day as his muscles experienced hypertrophy. He became an Olympic champion and the only man who could carry a 4-year-old bull, due to his discovery of muscle fatigue and hypertrophy (even though he lacked the technical vocabulary to describe his methods in those terms).[64]

Resistance training worked for Milo, and resistance training is what continues to work today. Milo's muscles resisted against a cow, but his muscles didn't know it was a cow. His muscles just knew there was a stimulus in the environment that caused them to fatigue. A cow will work great for this purpose, but so will dumbbells, barbells, boulders, body weight, heavy bands, sand bags, kettlebells, or anything else capable of creating muscle fatigue.

This is why aerobic exercise as performed by most people is quite useless. We saw in the first part of this book why it is ineffective for losing weight, but it's also ineffective at building muscle because it doesn't create enough muscle fatigue (even if you experience cardiovascular fatigue). Running on a treadmill, for instance, doesn't create enough resistance for your muscles to adequately fatigue your type 1 fibers, leading to type 2 fiber recruitment, and thereby initiate muscle growth. Ever notice how the guys using free weights have muscles, but the treadmill jockeys don't? I wish someone had told me this years ago. I just thought as long as I was

---

[64] https://jamesclear.com/milo

doing something under the broad category of fitness that muscles would be a by-product, but this simply isn't true.

Resistance training is uniquely capable of transforming our bodies and our health. In a study titled "Resistance training is medicine: effects of strength training on health,"[65] the authors concluded the following:

- "Ten weeks of resistance training may increase lean weight by 1.4 kg, increase resting metabolic rate by 7%, and reduce fat weight by 1.8 kg."

- "Benefits of resistance training include improved physical performance, movement control, walking speed, functional independence, cognitive abilities, and self-esteem."

- "Resistance training may assist prevention and management of type 2 diabetes by decreasing visceral fat, reducing HbA1c, increasing the density of glucose transporter type 4, and improving insulin sensitivity."

- "Resistance training may enhance cardiovascular health, by reducing resting blood pressure, decreasing low-density lipoprotein cholesterol and triglycerides, and increasing high-density lipoprotein cholesterol. Resistance training may

---

[65] https://www.ncbi.nlm.nih.gov/m/pubmed/22777332

promote bone development, with studies showing 1% to 3% increase in bone mineral density."

- "Resistance training may be effective for reducing low back pain and easing discomfort associated with arthritis and fibromyalgia and has been shown to reverse specific aging factors in skeletal muscle."

It's quite astounding how powerful resistance training is for transforming many aspects of our health.

The Best Form of Resistance Training

So what is the best form of resistance training? Please, be aware of the religious debate that we are entering. This is a Catholic vs. Protestant situation. All sides have their poster boys (the guys that got ripped using their form of training), each side has their science (the number of articles flying around touting this method vs. that method is staggering), and all parties warn you about doing it the *other* way—you will get hurt, or get bored, or not progress, etc.

The bottom line is that muscle fatigue and resistance training is where the magic is. How you choose to create that fatigue is a preference, nothing more, nothing less. There are two kinds of people in the world: those who understand muscle fatigue and those who don't. Let's not further subdivide things arbitrarily.

One popular method of resistance training is the use of dumbbells. Like a growing calf, you can increase the load easily by grabbing a heavier dumbbell, and because of their shape, they are easy to manipulate in your hand. Dumbbells have stood the test of time as a legitimate form of resistance training, and amazing bodies have been built using them.

The use of barbells is another favorite form of resistance training. This setup consists of a bar, a rack of some kind, and an assortment of plates that can be put on the bar. Like dumbbells, it's easy to progressively increase the weight to ensure muscle fatigue as you develop. The bar allows you to train with both hands manipulating the same weight, creating a stability that lends itself well to deadlifts, squats, and bench presses. Again, amazing bodies have sworn by barbells as the best form of resistance training.

Another massively popular tool for resistance training are the Nautilus-style machines. These are the machines you see at a gym with the stack of weights and a pin that lets you choose how much you are going to lift. There is a machine built to isolate almost any muscle in your body, and some gyms are replacing their barbells and dumbbells in order to go the machine route.

If modern machines are not for you, you can go to Scotland or Iceland; They both have a history of stone lifting. Their countryside is scattered with incredibly heavy stones that each create a unique challenge for the lifter. These stones are in some ways an anti-gym. As opposed to gym equipment, these stones are not uniform, they are outside, and they are dirty. Guess what? They still create resistance, muscle fatigue, and hypertrophy.

If you prefer one form of resistance training to another, keep going in that direction. You like machines? Great. You like dumbbells or kettlebells? Great. Consistency will trump novelty and variety. By being consistent with a routine that creates true muscle fatigue throughout your life, you'll be much closer to your goals than by sitting around and debating the best form of resistance. Stop debating and go grab something heavy.

With all that being said, my favorite form of resistance training is body weight exercises, also known as calisthenics. During body weight exercises you are literally using your own body as the weight to create muscle fatigue. Your muscles don't know if you are lifting a cow, or yourself, but both will work just fine. I prefer this style of resistance training for three main reasons: portability, efficiency, and cost.

The first reason I prefer body weight exercises is portability. If you travel a lot, you know how important the portability factor is. I sometimes travel for work, and most hotel gyms (if they even have one) lack the necessary equipment. I also travel for months each summer with my family on adventures all over the world. This means (depending on the location) that I am away from civilization for extended periods of time with no access to any gym or any modern equipment. As I write this, I am actually in the middle of the jungle in Latin America. Given the sheer size and weight of plates and dumbbells it would have been impossible to bring them along with me. Therefore, I don't have many options.

The second reason I prefer body weight resistance training is that it is efficient. Since my body is always with me, I never have to drive to the gym and waste that time in my already busy life. I often do push-ups on the kitchen floor as my steak and eggs are cooking for breakfast. I can knock out some squats in my office when I need a break from work. I don't have to bother with the machines at the gym: jumping from one to another, fiddling around with knobs and settings, waiting for my turn with the dumbbells, waiting for a bench to open up, wiping down my seat with disinfectant for the next person, then shower and drive home. My workouts are incredibly efficient, and I can fit them in whenever. If you are young and single and you want to spend hours at the gym, then go for it. I don't.

The third reason I prefer body weight exercises is the cost. Gym memberships are not cheap. If you look into creating your own home gym, the financial costs can also add up quickly. Even more substantial is the space it will cost. To get all the gear you need equals quite an investment in both money and square footage. If you are really into working out and it is a significant part of your identity, then a home gym might be perfect for you. To me, working out isn't my life. I don't want gym equipment filling up entire rooms in my house.

I want the most efficient way to build muscle. That's why it's easy for me to bypass the gym, free weights, and machines and all that these things entail. Body weight is a perfect alternative that fits my preference for minimalism and my desire to travel. If you are driven by similar motives, keep reading. You'll be pleasantly surprised by the true power of body weight exercises.

A Brief History of Calisthenics

Let's take a brief look at the origins and history of body weight training to examine why this form of resistance exercise stood the test of time. Body weight training, or *calisthenics* as it's also called, comes from two Greek words. It comes from the word *kallos* (κάλλος), meaning "beauty" and the word *sthenos* (σθένος), meaning "strength." Calisthenics was originally used in ancient Greece as a way to train for war. According to the historian Herodotus, Xerxes sent spies to the Spartan camp and saw them performing calisthenics during the Battle of Thermopylae (highlighted in the movie *300*).[66] The legendary professional football player and MMA fighter, Herschel Walker, also used calisthenics to build his world-class body. According to the website, the *Art of Manliness*, "As a chubby adolescent, at first Walker couldn't do any push-ups at all. He slowly worked his way up to 25 by doing as many as he could in a stretch, taking a 10-15 second break, and then doing some more until he hit that number. Using the same approach, he worked up to doing 50 push-ups a night, then 100. Slowly he increased his reps until he was doing 2,000 a day as a young man . . ."[67] It is also recorded that Walker did 1,500 pull-ups a day and up to 1,000 squats a day.

Calisthenics, specifically push-ups, are even used as an important component of the CFT (Combat Fitness Test) in the United States Marine Corps, the ACFT (Army Combat Fitness Test) for the United States Army, and the PRT (Physical Readiness Test) in the United States Navy.

---

[66] https://www.bbc.com/reel/video/po757qbx/how-ancient-greeks-trained-for-war

[67] https://www.artofmanliness.com/articles/the-herschel-walker-workout

The Science of Calisthenics

Calisthenics were good enough for the Spartans, Herschel Walker, and continue to be for multiple branches of the United States armed forces, but a new study shows that push-ups might also be an indicator for heart disease risk.

A paper published in the *Journal of the American Medical Association* reported that, "This longitudinal cohort study of 1104 occupationally active adult men found a significant negative association between baseline push-up capacity and incident cardiovascular disease risk across 10 years of follow-up. Participants able to complete more than 40 push-ups were associated with a significant reduction in incident of cardiovascular disease event risk compared with those completing fewer than 10 push-ups."[68] This means that your ability to do push-ups significantly correlates with your risk of cardiovascular disease.

Studies also show how favorably body weight exercises compare to their more complicated alternatives. Dr. Naoki, from the Department of Training Science at Nippon Sport Science University in Japan, published a study where he compared the push-up to the bench press because he wanted to know which was better for muscle growth (hypertrophy). He concluded that

---

[68] https://jamanetwork.com/journals/jamanetworkopen/fullarticle/2724778

"Push-up exercise with similar load to 40%1RM bench press is comparably effective for muscle hypertrophy and strength gain over an 8-week training period." Again, this just shows that resistance training in general is what is most important, not necessarily the method of resistance. Push-ups are comparable to a bench press.[69]

Another meta-analysis that reviewed twenty-one different published studies attempted to discover which was better for strength and hypertrophy, high loads or low loads of resistance during training. Dr. Schoenfeld concluded that "The findings indicate that maximal strength benefits are obtained from the use of heavy loads while muscle hypertrophy can be equally achieved across a spectrum of loading ranges."[70] This means that body weight exercises, which use a low load compared to other methods of resistance, are comparable to using heavy loads for the sake of hypertrophy (muscle growth), which is our goal.

Just because we have an endless array of modern options to build our bodies doesn't mean that the old school methods are broken. Your body is your best gym—it's always open, it's never crowded, it's anywhere you are, it costs nothing, and it can produce incredible results.

---

[69] https://www.ncbi.nlm.nih.gov/pmc/articles/PMC5812864

[70] https://www.ncbi.nlm.nih.gov/m/pubmed/28834797

Strength to Weight Ratio

Body weight exercises are unique because they are the only form of resistance training that relies heavily on your strength-to-weight ratio. The lighter you are, relative to your strength, the easier calisthenics will be. Your body fat percentage is an excellent indicator of how difficult body weight exercises will be for you.

One of my sons, who is five, can currently do as many pull-ups as Brian Shaw, four-time winner of the World's Strongest Man competition. Shaw can only do six pull-ups despite literally being one of the strongest humans on the planet.[71] How is this possible? Shaw has a bad strength-to-weight ratio for body weight exercises. He is obviously strong, but we are not going for strong alone; we are going for lean. To be lean we want the right mix of muscle and body fat percentage. That's the key to looking good and feeling good.

This is why I love body weight training. It is the only kind of resistance training that actually forces you to have an aesthetically pleasing body to do the exercises successfully. If you overeat on fat and carbs and use only dumbbells, you'll become very strong and very overweight and not crack The Naked Code. However, if you stick with calisthenics, it forces you to have a low

---

[71] https://www.youtube.com/watch?v=35Gf5Gmm9Mw

body fat percentage while you are building muscle, which creates the physique we want.

I recommend losing most of your extra fat before you focus on building muscle with calisthenics for a few different reasons. First, this will give you a better strength-to-weight ratio as a starting point. Second, exercise is a stressor on the body, and stress is detrimental to weight loss.[72] Third, this will give your body the necessary time to get through the transition period of burning fat for fuel, instead of carbs. This will help you have more energy during your workouts. If you try to exercise during the transition, you might feel a lack of energy as your body is adjusting to the new macronutrients. I would take the first few months (or more, depending on how much you need to lose), to get your body fat percentage down. Then I would start calisthenics.

Once you reach about twenty percent body fat as a man, or twenty-five percent body fat as a woman, you are ready to start building muscle. Most people can achieve fifteen percent body fat or less if they consistently follow The Naked Code, but at twenty to twenty-five percent is a good point to incorporate exercise into your routine. Listen to your body. You will likely feel the urge to build your muscles as your body fat percentage decreases and you feel more capable and mobile.

---

[72] https://www.ncbi.nlm.nih.gov/pmc/articles/PMC6296480

There are a few reasons why I prefer to use body fat percentage as our primary indicator of health and progress, instead of using overall weight or BMI (body mass index). Overall weight is not a good metric for health because we never want to just lose weight, but rather, our goal should be to lose fat. We don't want to lose muscle, but an overall weight loss goal ignores this fact. Also, you can radically alter your body composition, and look incredible naked, without losing any weight at all, if you lose fat and gain muscle. Likewise, BMI is not helpful in assessing our health because once you start building muscle you could have a BMI score that categorizes you as obese because of the extra muscle mass, despite being in incredible shape.

Body fat percentage is the ideal metric for our goals since it informs us of how much fat we have on our bodies as opposed to lean body mass (muscle, blood, organs, bones, etc.). The easiest way to measure body fat percentage is to buy a scale that automatically calculates it. They are not that expensive (they start at about twenty-five dollars), and they are accurate enough for our purposes. You can find them on Amazon by searching "body fat percentage scale."

Using the graphic below set a goal body weight percentage that you want to achieve. Goals are important because they motivate us to achieve greater things then would without them. Don't be afraid to set a difficult goal. You will probably be surprised at how much your body can change in a three month period.

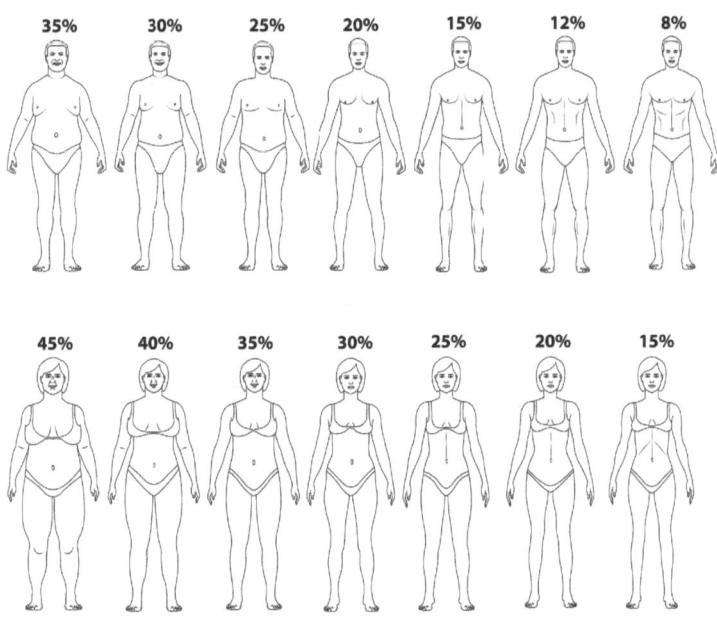

The Four Essential Body Weight Exercises

There are four body weight exercises that work virtually every muscle in your body. They are the push-up, the pull-up, the knee raise, and the squat. If our goal is to create fatigue in our muscle tissue, the most efficient way to do that would be to do compound exercises that engage more than one muscle group at a time. That is what these four exercises accomplish. Between the four of them, virtually every muscle will experience fatigue.

Another way to think about these exercises is to see them through the lens of your planes of motion. If you distill all your bodily movements down to their essence, the human body has four main movements: it pushes things away from the body, it pulls things closer to the body, it hinges at the hips, and it squats down. These encompass all of your large bodily joints or possible movements. Let's look at each of these planes of motion a little more.

Your body can only push things away in a few different ways. It can push things overhead, it can push things perpendicular to your body, or it can push things down. You can't effectively push things behind you (your arms don't work that way). These degrees of motion are what make up all the different pushing exercises. Pushing something upward is a shoulder press. Pushing something perpendicular to your body is a bench press. Pushing something down is a dip. While it's true that different degrees of arm rotation will work muscles in slightly different ratios, all pushes utilize the same muscles.

Since all pushing exercises are attempting to create fatigue in the same muscles, it makes sense why the push-up is one of our essential body weight exercises. A push-up will create fatigue and hypertrophy in all the pushing muscles of your upper body: pectorals, deltoids, and triceps.

Likewise, if we consider the planes of motion in use when pulling things toward your body, there are only a few options: You can pull things down toward your body, you can pull things perpendicular to your body, or you can pull things off the ground. Again, these make up all of the pulling exercises. Pulling something down is a lat pulldown, pulling something perpendicular to your body is a seated row, and pulling something off the ground is a barbell row. All pulls work the same muscles. The pull-up is one of our essential body weight exercises because it will create fatigue and hypertrophy in all the muscles responsible for these actions in your upper body: deltoids, biceps, lats, and trapezius.

Another plane of motion that the human body exhibits is the hip hinge. We have the ability to move our bodies like a hinge at our hips. We can bend to both sides slightly, and we can bend to the front with quite a bit of mobility. These represent the various core exercises that are possible. Bending to the sides could be a barbell side bend exercise. Bending toward the front could be a sit-up or crunch. All of the exercises that utilize the hip hinge target the abdominal muscles.

Given the fact that all hip hinge exercises target the abs, it makes sense that the knee raise is one of our essential body weight exercises. A knee raise will create fatigue and hypertrophy in all of the core muscles of your upper body. An added benefit is that the knee raise also targets your forearms and hands since you are forced to hang on the bar for extended periods of time (even longer than when doing pull-ups), and this is very taxing on your forearms and grip strength. Some people actually report that their forearms or hands give out before their abs do when executing knee raises, proving that it is a great exercise for those muscles. The knee raise targets the following muscle groups: abdominals and forearms.

The last multi-joint movement is the squat. There are not a lot of variations or degrees of rotation for this body movement. A squat is a squat. You can do squats inverted on a leg-press machine, or you can do squats upright with an Olympic bar and plates. But again, for our purposes, the body weight squat will be perfect for hitting the same muscles. All squatting movements target the glutes, quads, hamstrings, and calves.

If you combine all four of these body weight exercises into your routine, you will be hitting every single major muscle in your body. The push-up, pull-up, knee raise, and squat combine to target the following muscle groups: pectorals, deltoids, triceps, abdominals, forearms, hands, biceps, lats, trapezius, glutes, thighs, hamstrings, and calves.

So why do people go to the gym and jump around to ten different machines to get a total-body workout? Maybe they don't know there is an easier way, or maybe they enjoy the experience of being at the gym and exercising as a hobby. I can't speak for them. For me, doing four body weight movements seems like the obvious choice.

You might be wondering if you should incorporate other body weight exercises into your routine besides these four. Sure, you can, but you don't have to for the sake of looking good naked. This is enough for you to hit every major muscle and reach the goal of an aesthetic body. I would keep things simple since you're less likely to follow complicated schemes consistently.

These four body weight exercises make up the second half of The Naked Code. "3 PPKS" stands for three days a week of push-ups, pull-ups, knee raises, and squats. I'll go through the exact routine later, but for now just know that if you eat more protein than carbs and fat combined (P > C + F) and if you do three days a week of push-ups, pull-ups, knee raises, and squats (3 PPKS), that you have all of the information necessary to transform your body.

The Essence of Muscle Growth

- Our muscles are made up of different kinds of fibers (type 1, type 2A, type 2B, and type 2X).

- Type 1 fibers handle our daily activities, and type 2 fibers handle situations that require more force.

- Type 2B and type 2X fibers are the largest fibers and will decide the size and shape of our muscles.

- We grow our muscle fibers by fatiguing them.

- Our body uses type 2B and type 2X muscle fibers only after type 1 fibers are fatigued.

- The best way to fatigue our type 1 fibers (and eventually our type 2 fibers) is through resistance training.

- Calisthenics is resistance training that can fatigue every major muscle in our body with four exercises.

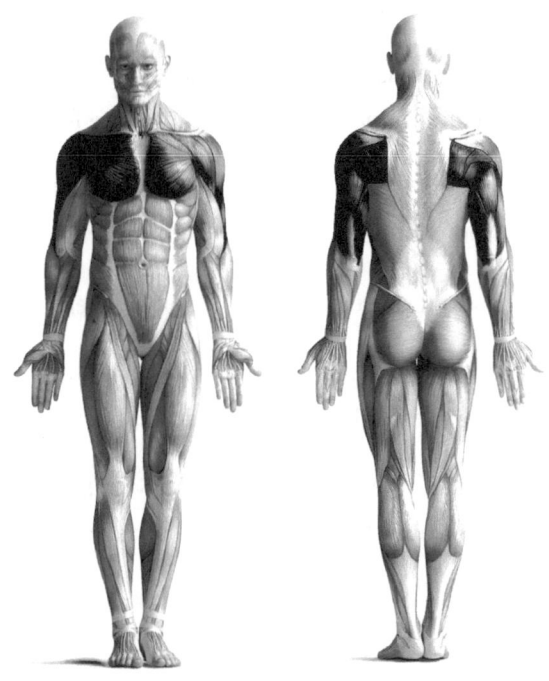

A **push-up** will create fatigue and hypertrophy in all of the pushing muscles of your upper body: **pectorals, deltoids, and triceps.**

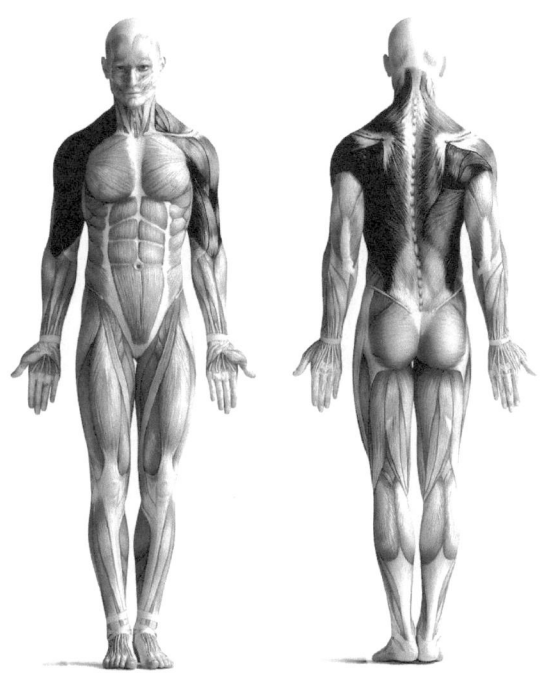

The **pull-up** will create fatigue and hypertrophy in all the pulling muscles of your upper body: **deltoids, biceps, lats, and trapezius.**

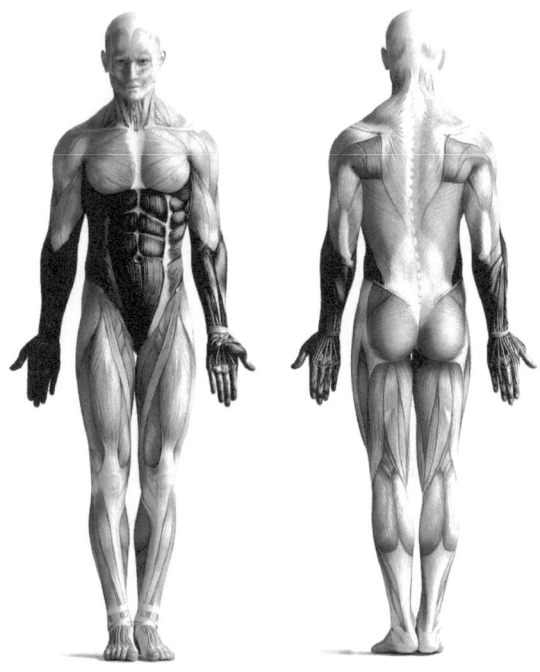

A **knee raise** will create fatigue and hypertrophy in your hands and forearms and the core muscles of your upper body: **abdominals.**

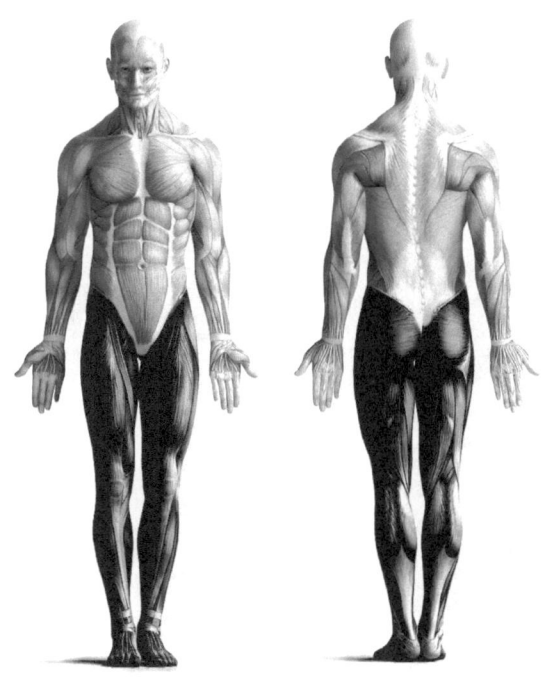

The **squat** will create fatigue and hypertrophy in all the leg muscles of your upper body: **glutes, quads, hamstrings, and calves.**

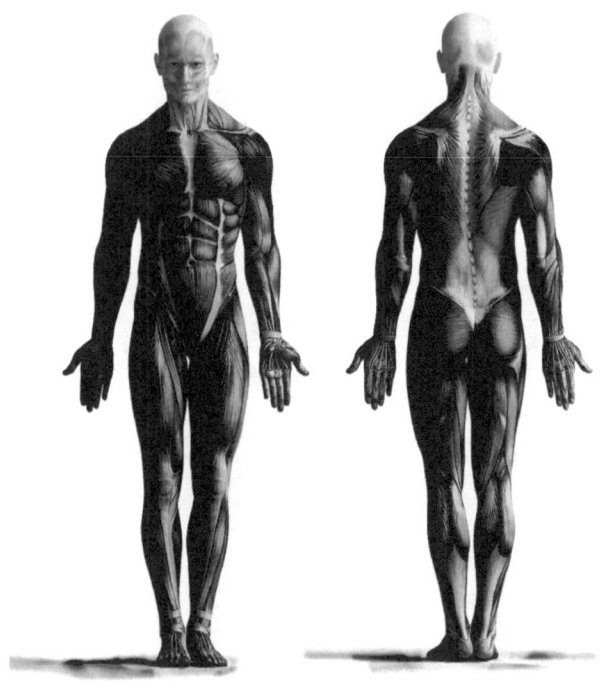

The **pull-up, push-up, knee raise, and squat** combine to create fatigue and hypertrophy in all the major muscles of your body: **pectorals, deltoids, triceps, abdominals, forearms, biceps, lats, trapezius, glutes, thighs, hamstrings, and calves.**

CHAPTER 4

THE REVERSE FIBONACCI WORKOUT

The Problem with Defined Programs

Now that you know the mechanics of muscle growth, it's time to learn a practical routine that lets you put all of the elements into practice. This is similar to how you learned the science of weight loss first and then learned how to eat your meals in a practical fashion. I think we should always know the *why* before the *how*.

If you've been around resistance training for very long, you've heard of "sets" and "reps." A "rep" is an individual instance of a movement. One push-up would be a single rep. A "set" is a series of reps that are completed without breaking form or stopping. Ten push-ups done in a row are one set of ten reps.

Many fitness programs advocate for performing exercises for a certain number of sets and reps. For instance, there is a popular program called 5x5, which gets its name from the fact that it teaches people to do five sets of five reps for each movement.

The problem with predefining how many sets and reps you should do of the four calisthenics exercises from the last chapter (PPKS) is that it may not align with your current ability. I can't tell you to do five sets of five push-ups if you can currently only do three push-ups total. Many people can't even do a single push-up, so how would they even get started? Do you see the dilemma?

I love calisthenics because of how accessible the movements are for almost everyone. With just a pull-up bar you can literally grow every major muscle in your body. I don't want to take something so accessible and restrict it by asking you to do things that are impossible.

Instead of telling you to do a certain number of sets and reps, I'm going to show you how to make progress regardless of where you are starting. This flexibility allows The Naked Code to work for individuals who have never worked out before, or for those who are already fit. However, before we get into the details, I want you to understand how progression works in general.

Understanding Progression

Plato once said, "Never discourage anyone who continually makes progress, no matter how slow . . . even if that someone is yourself!" This quote embodies the ethos of progressive training. It is possible, no matter where you are currently at, to make small steps that will lead toward incredible achievements.

To fully comprehend progressive training, I want you to think about the last film that you watched in the theater. Did you know that you were actually just watching a really fast PowerPoint presentation? Despite what you may remember, you weren't watching anything move on the screen, you were just watching a bunch of slides.

A film is actually just a series of static images, and if the images are cycled through fast enough, your brain interprets the still images as one continuous motion. A film is usually twenty-four FPS (frames per second), which means that during every single second you are actually seeing twenty-four different still images flash before your eyes. Twenty-four is an important number because if you are only shown twenty-three frames per second, the gaps between images are too large, and you start seeing the still images instead of motion. The fewer frames per second you are shown, the more your brain is incapable of filling in the gaps. Your brain is hardwired to create motion if the gaps are small enough.

So why are the visual mechanics of movies so important to our discussion? Because this is how progress works in every area of life, including fitness. You can create a fluid motion between almost any two points (like the beginning of a movie and the end of a movie) if you have enough tiny steps between the beginning and the end. Your brain and your body are capable of making progress right now, quite naturally, if the steps of your progression are close enough together. Progress is the ability to achieve big things through incredibly small steps.

People often fail at making progress because they try to get from A to Z by making large jumps in their ability, and the illusion of motion is broken. If you are out of shape and you try to get to ten push-ups within a week, you will probably fail, you'll get frustrated, and you'll ultimately give up. Trying to make progress too fast is unwise. However, if you aim for gradual progress over time, you will actually reach your goals instead of burning out.

We live in a microwave culture. We want our food cooked in five minutes, and we want a better body in ten minutes. There are no shortcuts in The Naked Code, but there are some principles that can change your life. One of these principles is the importance of consistency and progression. I don't care what your current capabilities are if you are willing to be consistent in your workouts and if your workouts continue to progress. If you do these two things, you will be creating a body that you are proud of. It won't happen overnight, but it will happen. Progress is the key.

The Progression of Movements

There are two kinds of progression that you must make to crack The Naked Code. There is a progression of movements and a progression of reps. We'll deal with reps in the next section, but here we will go through the progression of movements.

The pull-up is the hardest of the four body weight movements, so we'll start with it as a way to understand movement progressions. If you grab a bar and try to do a pull-up right now you can probably pull your body up a few inches. Unless you are currently working out regularly, I doubt you'll be able to do a single rep. So how do you even get started with this exercise? Progression of movements.

You don't start out trying to do regular pull-ups. Instead, you might start out by doing Australian pull-ups. These are pull-ups where your feet are resting on something to take some of the weight off your muscles. You could do Australian pull-ups using the edge of a table or a low pull-up bar, with your feet resting on the floor. You could also do Australian pull-ups on a regularly sized bar with your feet resting on a chair.

These movements develop the correct muscles until you can eventually do a real pull-up.

When I started this journey, I couldn't do a single real push-up with good form. Honestly, there was a part of me that wanted to give up before I even started. It felt embarrassing to do push-ups on my knees, especially since I've always heard those referred to as girl push-ups.

Well, I swallowed my pride, and I started doing knee push-ups on my office floor, despite being a male in my thirties. Guess what I found out that day? Nobody cares. The whole debate was in my head because, in reality, nobody cares what I do to workout. By starting with the correct movement, I was laying the right foundation. Here is the progression for each exercise:

Pull-up Progression

1: Dead Hang

Simply hang from a pull-up bar as long as you can without moving. This is one rep of the dead hang.

2: Negative Pull-ups

Use a regularly sized bar and with an overhand or underhand grip that is shoulder-width apart or a little more, use a chair to get your chin to the bar. Then, without using the chair, lower yourself down from the bar as slowly as you possibly can.

3: Australian Pull-ups

With hands shoulder-width apart or a little more, grab the edge of a table or a short bar, and do a pull-up with your body perfectly straight and your feet touching the ground. A regularly sized bar and a chair will also work. Do not use momentum.

4: Pull-ups

Use a regularly sized bar and, with an overhand or underhand grip that is shoulder-width apart or a little more, raise your chin to the bar and lower yourself. Do not use momentum.

Push-up Progression

1: Wall Push-ups

Lean against a wall, put your hands shoulder-width apart, and lower your body toward the wall and back again. Your elbows should almost pinch your ribs and your body should be straight. Do not use momentum.

2: Knee Push-ups

With your knees on the ground, put your hands shoulder-width apart and lower your body until your nose almost touches and then push back up again. Your elbows should almost pinch your ribs and your body should be straight. Don't use momentum.

3: Half Push-ups

With your feet on the ground, put your hands shoulder-width apart on the ground and lower your body until you are half way down and then back again. Your elbows should almost pinch your ribs and your body should be straight. Do not use momentum.

4: Push-ups

With your feet on the ground, put your hands shoulder-width apart on the ground and lower your body until your nose almost touches and then push back up again. During the movement your elbows should almost pinch your ribs and your body should be perfectly straight. Do not use momentum.

Knee Raise Progression

1: Floor Knee Raises

Lay flat on your back with your hands at your side, and keep your legs perfectly straight on the ground. Slowly raise your knees toward your chest and then slowly lower your knees and straighten your legs back out again. Don't let your feet touch the ground in between reps and do not use momentum.

2: Floor Leg Raises

Lay flat on your back with your hands at your side, and keep your legs perfectly straight. Slowly raise your legs off the ground until they are at a ninety-degree angle with the floor and then slowly lower them again. Don't let your feet touch the ground in between reps, and do not use momentum.

3: Seated Knee Raises

Sit on a bench and grab the edge of the bench with your hands for stability. Lean back and pick your feet up off the ground so that your body forms a straight line. Tuck your knees toward your chest and then straighten your body again without touching the floor with your feet.

4: Knee Raises

Hang from the pull-up bar with hands shoulder-width apart. Raise your knees up in the air until they are parallel with your waist and lower them again. Do not use momentum.

Squat Progression

1: Chair Squats
With your feet shoulder-width apart and your heels on the ground, sit in a chair with your back straight. Without using your hands, stand up again. Do not use momentum.

2: Wall Squats
With your feet shoulder-width apart and your heels on the ground, lean your back against a wall. Slide down the wall without using your hands until it looks like you are sitting on an invisible chair. Then raise your body back to the starting position.

3: Split Squats
Take a step forward so that one foot is in front of you and the other foot is behind you. Keep your front foot flat on the ground, and squat down until your other knee almost touches the ground. Your back foot should bend. Then raise up again to your starting position. Then do the same movement with the other leg.

4: Squats
With your feet shoulder-width apart and your heels on the ground, lower your body down until your thighs are parallel with the floor and then return to your standing position. Do not use momentum.

The Progression of Reps

The same way that there is a smart progression of movements, there is also a smart progression of reps. If you are doing the right movements, for the right number of reps, you will make progress.

The goal of rep progression is to fully fatigue your muscles during each workout. Studies show that if we work a muscle to failure, whether through light loads with high reps or heavy loads with low reps, that our type 2 muscle fibers are engaged and this promotes muscle growth.[73] Finding a rep progression that pushes you to failure, without expecting more, is hard to find. That's why I created my own flexible rep progression based on months of trial and error.

The Naked Code rep progression starts by doing as many reps as you can do, of the most advanced exercises that you can do. This gives you a baseline for that day's workout. Let's say you can do seven knee push-ups. That's your first set of the day.

Next, you are going to do more sets of that same movement until the total reps reaches the number you did in your first set. If you did seven in the first set, then all of the following sets need to add up to seven. Your sets and reps might look like this:

---

[73] https://physoc.onlinelibrary.wiley.com/doi/abs/10.1113/JP278056

- Set one: Seven reps
- Set two: Four reps
- Set three: Two reps
- Set four: One rep
- $4 + 2 + 1 = 7$

You are going to try to do as many reps as you can in each set, but your muscles are naturally going to get fatigued and the number of reps should be going down each time. If your rep count isn't going down in each set, then you probably didn't push yourself hard enough in your first set of the day. Also, it doesn't matter how many sets it takes to complete the workout. Maybe it only takes three sets, or maybe it will take five sets.

You will be surprised at how your first set of the day keeps increasing in reps over time. If you could only do seven reps to start the day, just wait a few workouts and you'll probably be doing eight reps to start the day (or more) of that same exercise.

One of the keys to properly fatiguing your muscles is to not allow yourself long breaks between your sets. We want our muscles to be fully fatigued, so the goal isn't to feel fresh again before starting another set. Catch your breath (for many people this is about thirty seconds). Then continue with another set.

This rep progression works because it pushes your muscles to the point of fatigue no matter who you are. If you actually do as many reps as you can in each and every set and you don't stop short when you could have done one or two more reps with good form, then you will fatigue your type 2B and type 2X muscle fibers, and your muscles will grow.

Once you are able to do ten reps in a single set of a given movement, it's time to move up to the next exercise in the progression. If you are able to do ten knee push-ups in a row, then you can probably do at least one real push-up with good form.

You might wonder how to handle movements when you can only do one rep total. Let's say you can only do one pull-up. You are going to do sets of one pull-up until you can't do any more sets. Then you're going to do the previous movement starting at your max and working down, like usual. Until you can do at least two reps of an exercise, I would recommend doing this so that you ensure your muscles are adequately fatigued. The reps and sets might look like this:

- Set one: One pull-up
- Set two: One pull-up
- Set three: Five Australian pull-ups
- Set four: Three Australian pull-ups
- Set five: Two Australian pull-ups

With The Naked Code rep progression you are always moving toward harder movements, and you are always progressing in the total number of reps that you are doing for each exercise. This ensures that you never stop advancing in your ability. If you follow this plan, you will get stronger every single day of your life. A plan like this is infinitely more intelligent than just mindlessly doing three sets of ten reps of whatever exercise you randomly select.

One of the reasons that this progression works so well is because it is loosely based on the Fibonacci sequence. As I was experimenting with different numbers of sets and reps I kept running into the same error. I needed a way to intelligently decrease my reps in each subsequent set during a workout. If I just maxed out by doing thirteen push-ups, there was a very small chance that I could do thirteen push-ups again during the second set that day. Then I remembered the Fibonacci sequence, which is a sequence of numbers where each number is the sum of the two preceding numbers. The beginning of the Fibonacci sequence is: 0, 1, 1, 2, 3, 5, 8, 13, 21 . . .

After looking at this sequence in reverse, it occurred to me that this would be an amazing basis for a rep progression chart. If I started by doing thirteen push-ups, I could probably do eight push-ups in my next set and five in my last set. If I started by doing five push-ups, I could probably do three push-ups in my next set and two in my last set. There is something powerful and elegant about making subsequent sets add up to the first set.

This idea was also buried in a quote about Herschel Walker from earlier in this book. He followed this same scheme to increase his reps: "He slowly worked his way up to 25 by doing as many as he could in a stretch, taking a 10-15 second break, and then doing some more until he hit that number."[74]

Workout Frequency

In terms of workout frequency, I recommend working out on a Monday, Wednesday, Friday schedule. According to Peter Tiidus, A. Russell Tupling, and Michael Houston, authors of *Biochemistry Primer for Exercise Science, 4th Edition*, "A number of studies have shown that resistance exercise results in increased rates of muscle-protein synthesis, about two to five fold after exercise for periods up to 48 hours before declining to baseline values."[75] This means that we have increased muscle repair for forty-eight hours after a workout, so we don't need to train every day to get results.

The days you rest are the days you are actually getting stronger. When you have fully fatigued all of your muscle fibers, your body spends the next forty-eight

---

74 https://www.artofmanliness.com/articles/the-herschel-walker-workout

75 https://us.humankinetics.com/blogs/excerpt/resistance-training-increases-the-rate-of-muscle-protein-synthesis

hours using the protein in your diet to repair your muscles and making them grow larger.

Some people get great results working out daily, and other people get great results working out only weekly, but I would use a Monday, Wednesday, Friday schedule as a starting point to learn what works best for you.

If you listen to your body, you will probably discover the right cadence for you. If you are still very sore from your last workout, you may need more recovery time. If you find yourself wanting to workout more, you may need to increase the frequency. So start with three days a week and then adjust as necessary.

This means that following The Naked Code workout schedule would look something like this:

Sunday: Off

Monday:
- Australian pull-ups (5, 3, 2)
- Knee push-ups (8, 5, 3)
- Knee raises (15, 9, 6)
- Split squats (9, 6, 3)

Tuesday: Off

Wednesday:
- Australian pull-ups (6, 4, 2)
- Knee push-ups (9, 5, 4)
- Knee raises (16, 10, 6)
- Split squats (10, 7, 3)

Thursday: Off

Friday:
- Australian pull-ups (6, 5, 1)
- Knee push-ups (10, 6, 4)
- Knee raises (17, 11, 6)
- Squats (1, 1, 1) + split squats (5, 3, 2)

Saturday: Off

You are only working out three times a week, and you are only doing four movements per workout. Every time you workout, you will be doing some version of the pull-up, push-up, knee raise, and squat exercises, depending on which movement you can currently do. You will also be doing more reps of each movement over time so that you are continuously pushing yourself within each of those movements.

Remember, once you can get to ten reps of a given movement, it's time to move on to the next movement. This will continue until you get to the unmodified version of the exercise. This is why the sample workout goes from split squats on Wednesday to real squats on Friday (while adding in split squats after doing as many sets of one-rep squats as possible). During the Wednesday workout, ten reps of split squats were completed, so it was time to progress.

The Naked Code workout only requires three days a week, and it only takes about twenty minutes per workout. You will be spending an hour or less a week to transform your life. I have three kids and I run multiple businesses, but even I can fit this in my schedule.

How to Break Plateaus

Depending on the specifics of your development, you might find that you are stuck on a certain number of max reps. Let's say you can do thirteen push-ups, but you are not able to move on to fourteen push-ups. There are a few things you can do to break a calisthenics plateau.

The first thing you can try is to slow down your reps so your muscles have more time under tension (TUT), to make sure they are fatigued enough to become stronger. You can also try decreasing your rest between sets for this same reason.

The second thing to try is performing the difficult exercises first. The longer into a workout you are, the less energy you'll have available. Do the exercises that are hardest for you first to try to break plateaus.

The third thing you can try when you are stuck is to increase or decrease your days of rest between workouts. Finding the right frequency can allow you to break plateaus since you are optimizing your recovery time.

Finally, when you do attempt to hit a new max for reps, don't be afraid to use rest/pause techniques. This means that you keep your form, but you pause for a few seconds in between reps to regain your energy. When you finally try to do fourteen push-ups again you might do twelve reps, rest for a few seconds while keeping form, and then try to achieve the last two reps.

Advancing to More Difficult Movements

Once you can do over 10 reps of each of the movements outlined in this book, you might want to progress to even more difficult versions of each of the exercises. By doing more difficult movements, you will keep your exercise time to a minimum, and it will challenge your abilities. I would highly recommend downloading an app titled "Working Out," created by calisthenics legend, Al Kavadlo. It is incredibly simple to use, and it will show you how to progress beyond the movements in this book. Al's YouTube videos are also worth checking out.

Keeping Track of Your Progress

There is a progress tracker in the back of this book so that you can record your key stats on a regular basis. It's important that you keep track of your progress because it will encourage momentum as you see how much you are actually improving.

My Final Thoughts

Do you ever notice how people who do yoga consider it a *practice*? It's a lifestyle. It's not a competition, and it definitely doesn't have an end point. They never finish yoga.

I think this same mindset would be beneficial for anyone utilizing The Naked Code. You are not going to finish. This is now a lifestyle, one that involves eating differently and doing resistance training. This is an ongoing part of your life now. This is not a phase you are going through. This is the new you.

I have achieved my results by considering this a practice. I didn't kill myself in the gym for a month and then quit. I didn't kill myself in the kitchen for a month and then quit. I did simple things consistently, and I understood the science behind what I was doing. It really isn't as difficult as you think, but it will require viewing this as your new life.

I recommend starting this new life as soon as possible. There is a Chinese proverb that says, "The best time to plant a tree was twenty years ago. The second best time is now." I wish I had been in shape a long time ago, but the day I did start was the second best option. I hope you consider starting this journey today. Having a healthy body will greatly contribute to your quality of life. Being overweight and being weak doesn't bring anyone joy. Invest in yourself so you'll have the energy and confidence to invest in those around you.

Transform your body and your health by eating more grams of protein than grams of carbs and fat combined and by doing three days a week of pull-ups, push-ups, knee raises, and squats. It's time to unlock The Naked Code:

P>C+F 3PPKS = LEAN

Checklist for Beginners

If you are ready to transform your body, but you are not sure where to begin, I made a checklist to help you out. These are the twenty-five things I would do, and the order I would do them in, to follow The Naked Code. Check off the items as you complete them.

☐ Decide you want to look good naked.

☐ Take a before picture that shows your extra weight.

☐ Buy a body fat percentage scale. You can find them on Amazon for about $25.

☐ Set a body fat percentage goal. Use the body fat percentage illustration earlier in this book.

☐ Write down your starting stats in the back of this back (ignore the exercise column for now).

☐ Shop for groceries and buy meat, eggs, and low-carb vegetables.

☐ Download MyFitnessPal and start tracking your meals. It will show you how many grams of protein you are eating each day compared to carbs and fat.

☐ Experiment with your meals until you are able to eat more grams of protein than carbs and fat combined.

☐ Don't eat cheat meals. It will just slow down your progress and make you crave junk food again.

☐ Salt your food generously.

☐ Don't cook in vegetable oils or seed oils. Use beef tallow, coconut oil, or extra virgin olive oil instead.

☐ Set a mini-goal of eating more grams of protein than carbs and fat combined for 7 days in a row to get in the habit of eating this way.

☐ Record your stats in the back of this book every week (ignore the exercise column for now).

☐ Take a progress photo every week when you record your stats.

☐ Get below twenty percent body fat if you are a man. Get below twenty-five percent body fat if you are a woman.

☐ Buy a pull-up bar that goes in your doorway. You can find them on Amazon for about $20.

☐ Discover which version of the four body weight exercises that you can currently do.

☐ Do a full workout using the four exercises that you can do, and use the reverse Fibonacci sequence for reps and sets.

☐ Do The Naked Code workout three times a week.

☐ Once you can do ten reps of an exercise in one set then progress to the next movement.

☐ Continue to eat more grams of protein than carbs and fat combined.

☐ Record your stats in the progress tracker in the back of this book every week but include your exercise stats now.

☐ Reach your ideal body fat percentage and feel like a rock star for accomplishing your goal.

☐ Now that you are lean, experiment with higher amounts of fat to keep your energy high and your muscles from breaking down. Continue to keep your carbs low.

☐ Email bronson.taylor@gmail.com and share your story (include photos and stats).

Did You Follow The Naked Code?

If you followed the advice in this book and finally lost the extra weight, gained muscle, and reclaimed your health, I want to hear from you. Send me your before and after photos, along with your personal Naked Code story to bronson.taylor@gmail.com. Every story has the ability to catalyze more people into taking action.

The Naked Code Progress Tracker

Date	Weight	BF %	Exercises & Max Reps

The Naked Code Progress Tracker

Date	Weight	BF %	Exercises & Max Reps

The Naked Code Progress Tracker

Date	Weight	BF %	Exercises & Max Reps

The Naked Code Progress Tracker

Date	Weight	BF %	Exercises & Max Reps

The Naked Code Progress Tracker

Date	Weight	BF %	Exercises & Max Reps

The Naked Code Progress Tracker

Date	Weight	BF %	Exercises & Max Reps

Made in United States
Troutdale, OR
06/28/2024

20877850R00094